COLLINS LIVING HISTORY

Native Peoples
of North America

Fiona Macdonald
Series editor: Christopher Culpin

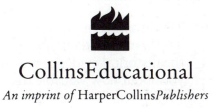

Collins Educational
An imprint of HarperCollinsPublishers

Contents

UNIT 1 The first Americans   page 6

UNIT 2 Peoples and places   16

UNIT 3 The old ways   24

UNIT 4 Contact and change   42

UNIT 5 Whose America?   52

Glossary   61

Index   63

attainment target 1

Questions aimed at this attainment target find out how much you know and understand about the past. Some questions are about how things were different in history: not only people's food, or clothes but their beliefs too. Others are about how things change through history, sometimes quickly, sometimes slowly, sometimes a little, sometimes a lot. Other questions ask you to explain why things were different in the past, and why changes took place.

attainment target 2

This attainment target is about understanding what people say about the past. Historians, as well as lots of other people, try to describe what the past was like. Sometimes they say different things. This attainment target is about understanding these differences and why they occur.

attainment target 3

This attainment target is about historical sources and how we use them to find out about the past. Some questions are about the historical evidence we can get from sources. Others ask you about how valuable this evidence might be.

Introduction

This book looks at the long history of the Native peoples of North America, from around 30,000 BC until AD 1900. During that time, unique and fascinating civilisations grew up in different regions of North America as separate groups, or nations, of Native peoples settled on the land. Although their lifestyles were different, all Native nations shared a respect for the natural world, and a belief in the powerful spirits that controlled it.

Over the centuries, Native cultures changed. Nations became rich and powerful, or were weakened by famine or disease. However, these changes were slight compared with the enormous impact made by Europeans on Native American ways of life, after explorers reached America in AD 1492. At first, Native nations were under pressure to trade with the Europeans. Later, Europeans wanted to take over Native lands. There were bitter, bloody wars, in which many Native people were killed. For a while, it looked as if Native American civilisation was at an end. But it has survived to win new respect and admiration from many people today.

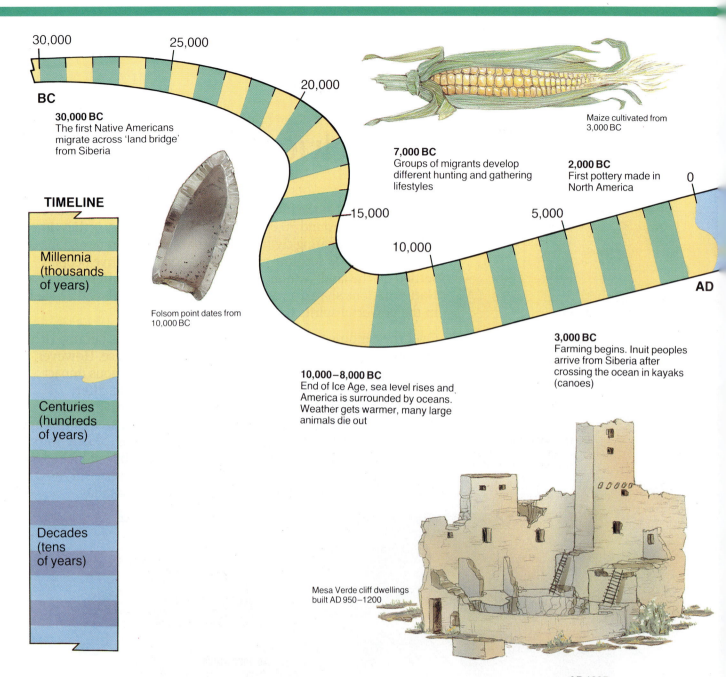

30,000   25,000
20,000

BC

30,000 BC
The first Native Americans
migrate across 'land bridge'
from Siberia

Maize cultivated from
3,000 BC

7,000 BC
Groups of migrants develop
different hunting and gathering
lifestyles

2,000 BC
First pottery made in
North America

0

15,000

10,000

5,000

AD

TIMELINE

Millennia
(thousands
of years)

Centuries
(hundreds
of years)

Decades
(tens
of years)

Folsom point dates from
10,000 BC

10,000–8,000 BC
End of Ice Age, sea level rises and
America is surrounded by oceans.
Weather gets warmer, many large
animals die out

3,000 BC
Farming begins. Inuit peoples
arrive from Siberia after
crossing the ocean in kayaks
(canoes)

Mesa Verde cliff dwellings
built AD 950–1200

AD 1885
Last great buffalo herd killed

AD 1890
Battle of Wounded Knee;
Native peoples defeated

AD 1910
Native population now less than
250,000

AD 1968
National Council for Indian
Opportunities set up

AD 1980
Native population now almost
1.5 million

As you read through this book and look at the
sources, you will find out about the beautiful and
impressive objects made by people from
different Native American cultures. You will also
be able to explore the hopes, fears and beliefs
shared by Native American people. This book
also shows how Native culture has been
misrepresented in the past, and how, more
recently, historians have tried to find better
ways of understanding its achievements. The
timeline on this page shows the long history of
Native peoples before the Europeans arrived and
the changes that affected Native lives after these
new migrants settled in North America.

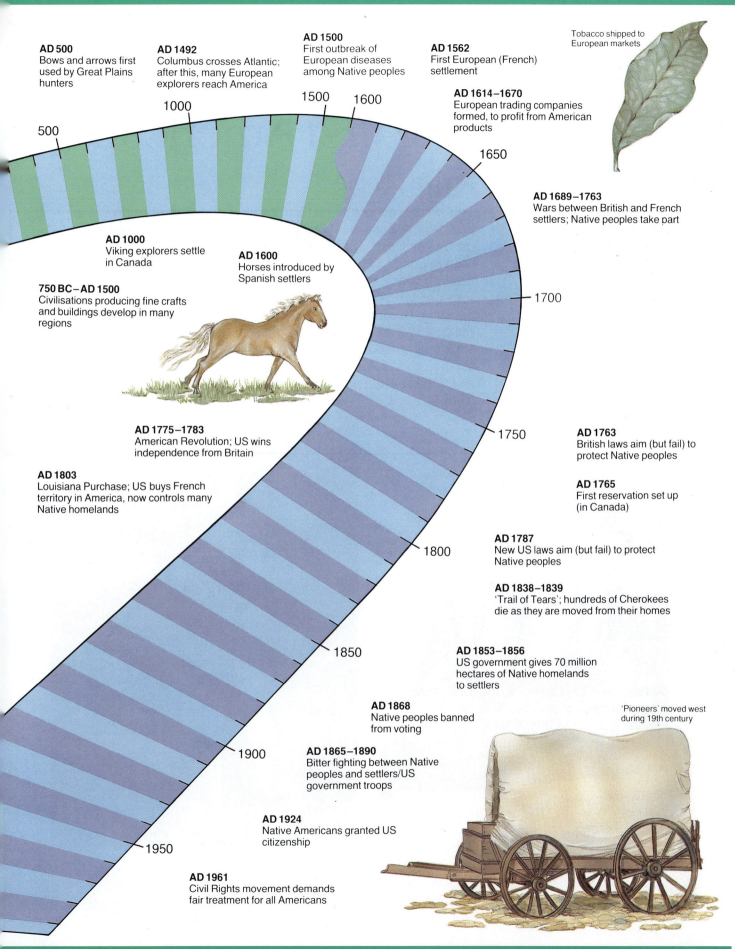

AD 500
Bows and arrows first used by Great Plains hunters

AD 1492
Columbus crosses Atlantic; after this, many European explorers reach America

AD 1500
First outbreak of European diseases among Native peoples

AD 1562
First European (French) settlement

Tobacco shipped to European markets

AD 1614–1670
European trading companies formed, to profit from American products

AD 1689–1763
Wars between British and French settlers; Native peoples take part

500

1000

1500

1600

1650

AD 1000
Viking explorers settle in Canada

AD 1600
Horses introduced by Spanish settlers

750 BC – AD 1500
Civilisations producing fine crafts and buildings develop in many regions

1700

AD 1775–1783
American Revolution; US wins independence from Britain

AD 1803
Louisiana Purchase; US buys French territory in America, now controls many Native homelands

1750

AD 1763
British laws aim (but fail) to protect Native peoples

AD 1765
First reservation set up (in Canada)

AD 1787
New US laws aim (but fail) to protect Native peoples

1800

AD 1838–1839
'Trail of Tears'; hundreds of Cherokees die as they are moved from their homes

AD 1853–1856
US government gives 70 million hectares of Native homelands to settlers

1850

AD 1868
Native peoples banned from voting

'Pioneers' moved west during 19th century

AD 1865–1890
Bitter fighting between Native peoples and settlers/US government troops

1900

AD 1924
Native Americans granted US citizenship

1950

AD 1961
Civil Rights movement demands fair treatment for all Americans

The first Americans

Native people

This book is about the history of the 'Native American people'. Normally, we use the word 'native' to mean somebody coming from a particular country, town or city. We could say that someone born in London is 'a native of London'. In the United States of America today, the words 'Native American' do not just mean someone who was born there. They have a different, more precise meaning. Usually, they describe someone who is descended from the people who were living in the Americas before European explorers arrived in 1492. So we could say that 'Native American' means 'original American' or 'first American'. Native American people have often described themselves in this way, as you can see from Source 1.

AIMS

In this unit we shall look at when and how the Native American people first settled in their homeland, and at the wide range of evidence available to tell us about their lives. We shall also look at some of the questions we face when trying to make sense of this evidence.

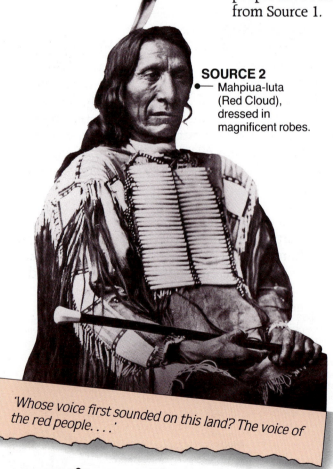

SOURCE 2
Mahpiua-luta (Red Cloud), dressed in magnificent robes.

'Whose voice first sounded on this land? The voice of the red people....'

SOURCE 1
These words were spoken by the Sioux Chief Mahpiua-luta (Red Cloud) in 1865.

SOURCE 3
Kaiar, a member of the Paiute nation, from Nevada, photographed in summer clothing in 1873.

One land, many peoples

Not all Native American peoples were the same. They belonged to many different nations (sometimes called 'tribes' in the past). They spoke different languages, wore different styles of clothes, ate different foods and lived in different types of houses. You can find out more about how they lived in units 2 and 3 of this book. Chief Mahpiua-luta (Red Cloud), who spoke the words in Source 1 and is pictured in Source 2, was a leader of one of the largest Native American nations – the Sioux. In Sources 3 and 4, you can see photographs of people from other Native American nations.

SOURCE 4
Women from the Navajo nation, Arizona, weaving blankets. This photograph was taken around 1868.

SOURCE 5
Traditional skills being taught to young Native American people in Florida today.

The vitality of our race still persists. . . . We are the original discoverers of this continent, and the conquerors of it from the animal kingdom, and on it first taught the arts of war and peace, and first planted the institutions of virtue, truth and liberty. The European nations found us here and were made aware that it was possible for men to exist and subsist here. The race that has rendered this service to the other nations of mankind cannot utterly perish.

SOURCE 6
Part of a speech made by Pleasant Porter, a leader of the Cree nation, in 1900.

Contact and catastrophe

The photographs shown in Sources 2, 3 and 4 were taken during the 19th century. At that time, some Native American people were still following their traditional ways of life. These had remained almost unchanged for centuries. But other Native American lifestyles had been dramatically altered by contact with white soldiers, traders and SETTLERS. By the beginning of the 20th century, Native American CIVILISATIONS had been almost completely destroyed in many parts of the USA.

Fortunately, some aspects of Native American culture have survived. Source 5 reminds us that love and respect for traditional knowledge and beliefs can be handed on from generation to generation. Source 6 tells us that some Native American leaders have been determined that their people shall not die out, and that their achievements shall not be forgotten.

1 Look at Sources 2 and 5. Both are photographs, but one is modern and one is over 100 years old. In what ways are the photographs similar? In what ways are they different? Can you suggest why?

2 What image of Native American people do you think the two photographers were trying to give? Write three words to describe the people in each picture.

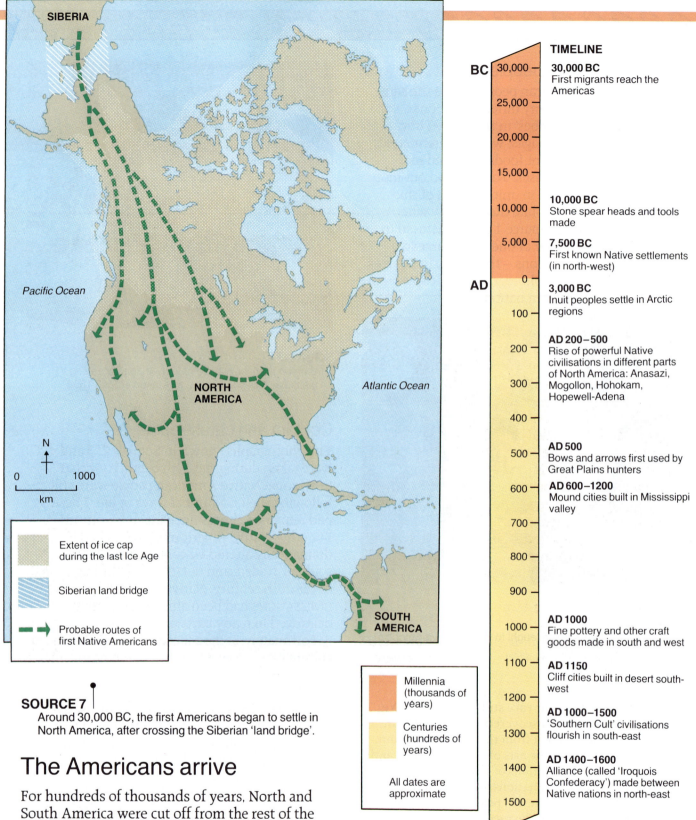

SIBERIA

Pacific Ocean

NORTH AMERICA

Atlantic Ocean

N

0   1000
km

Extent of ice cap
during the last Ice Age

Siberian land bridge

Probable routes of
first Native Americans

SOUTH AMERICA

SOURCE 7
Around 30,000 BC, the first Americans began to settle in
North America, after crossing the Siberian 'land bridge'.

TIMELINE

BC	
30,000	**30,000 BC** First migrants reach the Americas
25,000	
20,000	
15,000	
10,000	**10,000 BC** Stone spear heads and tools made
5,000	**7,500 BC** First known Native settlements (in north-west)
AD 0	**3,000 BC** Inuit peoples settle in Arctic regions
100	
200	**AD 200–500** Rise of powerful Native civilisations in different parts of North America: Anasazi, Mogollon, Hohokam, Hopewell-Adena
300	
400	
500	**AD 500** Bows and arrows first used by Great Plains hunters
600	**AD 600–1200** Mound cities built in Mississippi valley
700	
800	
900	
1000	**AD 1000** Fine pottery and other craft goods made in south and west
1100	**AD 1150** Cliff cities built in desert south-west
1200	
1300	**AD 1000–1500** 'Southern Cult' civilisations flourish in south-east
1400	**AD 1400–1600** Alliance (called 'Iroquois Confederacy') made between Native nations in north-east
1500	

Millennia
(thousands of
years)

Centuries
(hundreds of
years)

All dates are
approximate

The Americans arrive

For hundreds of thousands of years, North and
South America were cut off from the rest of the
world by deep, stormy oceans. No one lived
there. Around 80,000 BC, during the last Ice Age,
much of the Earth's water was frozen. Sea levels
fell, and large stretches of the seabed were
uncovered. A 'land bridge' – a strip of dry land –
was formed between the CONTINENTS of Asia and
America. It was about 1,600 kilometres long.

ARCHAEOLOGISTS think that the first people to set
foot in America travelled across this land bridge,
probably about 30,000 years ago (Source 7).
These first settlers were NOMADIC hunters. They
moved to the empty American continent,
following deer, tigers and BUFFALO.

Crossing the continent

Gradually, bands of these settlers travelled across the continent. Their descendants settled down and raised families. They became the Native American people. You can see some highlights in the development of the Native American civilisation in the timeline opposite.

The Inuit nation, who live in the cold Arctic north, arrived later. They crossed from Siberia to America in sealskin boats called kayaks around 3,000 BC. You can see an Inuit family in Source 8.

How do we know?

There are no written records to tell us when or how settlers first arrived in America. For years, many people refused to believe that the earliest Americans had arrived from Asia during the last Ice Age. They suggested a far more recent date.

Then, in 1926, archaeologists found the skeleton of a long-horned buffalo at Folsom in New Mexico. They also found a stone spear-head, which had killed the buffalo, stuck between its ribs (see Source 9). The spear-head had been carefully chipped and shaped by human hands, as you can see from Source 10. The hunter who threw the spear must have been living at the same time as the buffalo. The archaeologists knew that long-horned buffalo became extinct in America around 10,000 BC. So the first American hunters must have reached Folsom by then.

Since the spear-head was discovered, archaeologists have found cruder, simpler tools made of bone. They think these must date from even earlier centuries, when human skills were less well developed. Modern scientific tests have suggested that bone tools were made at least 29,000 years ago.

SOURCE 8
Inuit family outside their snow-covered camp, Baffin Island, Canada.

SOURCE 9
This stone spear-head was made by Native American people around 12,000 years ago. It was found between the ribs of a buffalo skeleton at Folsom, New Mexico.

SOURCE 10
Spear point from Folsom, New Mexico. It is 4.5 cm high and was made around 12,000 years ago.

ACTIVITY

Work in pairs. One of you is an archaeologist at Folsom, New Mexico. The other is a radio reporter. Work on an interview. The archaeologist should explain what has been found, what it means for the history of America and what it means for the history of Native Americans. The reporter should ask questions to help make the story as clear as possible.

Puzzles from the past

Native American civilisation has had a very long history. However, it is not always easy to understand the evidence which has been left behind. Native Americans did not develop a system of reading or writing until after they made contact with Europeans in the 16th century. So instead of written records, we have to use material remains to study much of the Native American past. What can we discover from this type of evidence?

SOURCE 11
A buffalo jump. Early hunters drove herds of wild buffalo over cliffs or into narrow gorges. Many animals died. Not all the meat could be eaten or stored for long, so much was left to rot.

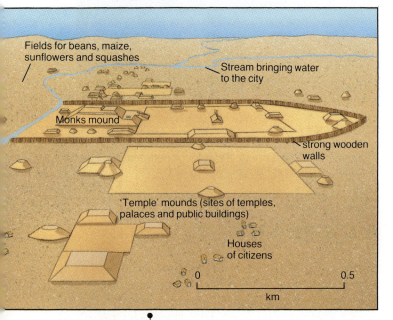

Fields for beans, maize, sunflowers and squashes

Stream bringing water to the city

Monks mound

strong wooden walls

'Temple' mounds (sites of temples, palaces and public buildings)

Houses of citizens

0   0.5

km

SOURCE 12
An artist's reconstruction of the great 'mound city' of Cahokia, Illinois, founded around AD 600. About 10,000 people lived here.

Everyday life

It is probably best to begin with evidence of people's daily lives. How, for example, did hunters get their food? Source 11 shows a buffalo jump, where mighty herds of buffalo were stampeded to death. What does this buffalo jump suggest about the bravery and team work of the men and women who planned it?

Now look at Source 12. It shows a modern reconstruction based on the remains of the great mound city at Cahokia, in present-day Illinois. What does it reveal about the wealth, power and technical skills of the people who built the city? What can pottery, basket work and metal work, shown in Sources 13 to 15, tell us about Native American craft skills and artistic tastes?

SOURCE 13
Pottery from Mimbres, New Mexico, made between AD 900 and 1200 by craftworkers from the Mogollon Native civilisation.

SOURCE 14
A basket made of dried grasses, decorated with feathers – made by women from the Pomo nation, California in the 19th century.

SOURCE 15 ———
This copper head was found in Oklahoma. It dates from about AD 1200 to 1350.

Without writing

Objects can tell us a great deal about everyday life, but it is much more difficult to use them to find out about what people thought, feared or believed. Sand pictures and TOTEM POLES (Source 16) portrayed magical or mysterious creatures. KACHINA DOLLS (Source 17) were made to look like guardian spirits. What clues about people's beliefs can you find from these objects? Why do you think they were made?

If we really want to understand what people thought or believed in the past, we need to listen to their own words. Fortunately, many ancient Native American traditions have been preserved in people's memories. In recent years, stories, MYTHS, songs, poems, prayers and historical records have all been written down (Source 18).

SOURCE 16
Bird and animal spirits, with ancestor figures, carved on a wooden totem pole from the north-west coastal region.

SOURCE 17 ———
This Native American painting shows Tawa, the sun kachina.

'Then, as we walked, there was a heaped up cloud ahead that changed into a TIPI, and a rainbow was the open door of it; and through the door I saw six old men sitting in a row. . . . And the oldest of these grandfathers spoke with a kind voice and said: 'Come right in and do not fear' . . . . So I went in and stood before the six, and they looked older than men can ever be – old like hills, like stars.'

SOURCE 18
Part of a vision, or dream, remembered by Hehaka Sapa (Black Elk) from the Sioux nation. He told his stories to a writer in 1932, when he was an old man.

> **1** Compare Sources 11, 12 and 13. Which do you think is most useful to historians studying the Native American past? What are the advantages and disadvantages of each source? What kinds of information can each source **not** give us?

Evidence from Europeans

All the sources on these two pages were produced by Europeans, between the 16th and early 19th centuries. This is only a short period compared with the 30,000 years of Native American history. However, even though this evidence comes from a limited time span, it has been very influential. It has shaped the way in which many people have viewed Native American civilisation. Can you think why?

European evidence is easier for us to understand. The written records are in European languages. Familiar European painting and drawing techniques are used in the visual sources. This familiarity can be dangerous. Just because we find European evidence easier to understand, it does not mean that it is more truthful or balanced.

Contrasting opinions

In Source 19, the writer describes Native American people almost as if they were animals. He was not alone in this attitude. During the 16th century, European church leaders even asked the question, 'Do Native American people have souls?' In other words, they were discussing whether Native American men and women were really 'proper' human beings.

Other Europeans were not so prejudiced. Travellers, like John White, were fascinated by Native American ways of life. In Source 20, you can see how carefully White portrayed the houses, fields and villages of Native American people. Today, we can use his paintings as a marvellous source of evidence. But at the time when they were produced, these paintings may have confirmed European attitudes that Native Americans were strange, different and EXOTIC (see Source 21).

SOURCE 20
The village of Secoton, Virginia, painted by John White around 1580.

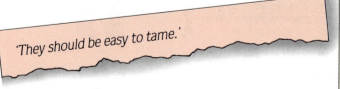

'They should be easy to tame.'

SOURCE 19
Part of a letter written by the 16th-century French traveller, Jacques Cartier, to King François I of France, who financed his journeys.

1 Look at Source 19. Today, we find the view it contains shocking. Can you suggest why people might have held views like this in the past?

2 Life in many 19th-century European cities was grim. Can you explain how this might have influenced the way travellers in America viewed Native lifestyles?

3 Look at Source 22. It was painted by a white American, educated in the European style. If you did not know who the artist was, what 'clues' might the painting give you about his origins and education?

SOURCE 21
From a European book about North America, published in 1700. The original caption was 'Savages fishing'.

Noble savages?

In the 19th century, artists and writers portrayed Native American people as 'noble savages', living pure, dignified lives, free from the problems of European civilisation. You can see two examples of this STEREOTYPE in Sources 22 and 23. This image may seem respectful and even flattering to Native American people, but it was also over-simplified. It was a patronising view which failed to realise that Native American culture was the product of many centuries of experience and INNOVATION. It assumed that European civilisation was more advanced. Native Americans were not considered as real people, but as exciting circus acts (see Source 24) or as glamorous figures in best-selling travellers' tales.

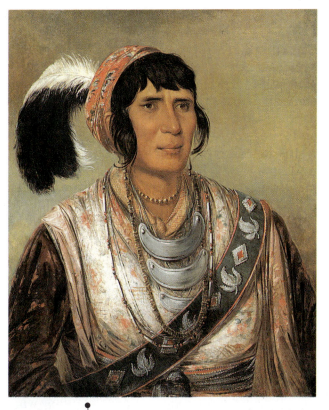

SOURCE 22
Osceola, a chief of the Seminole nation, who lived in Florida. Painted by the European-American artist and explorer, George Catlin, in 1838.

'The several tribes of Indians inhabiting the regions of the Upper Missouri . . . are undoubtedly the finest looking, best equipped, and most beautifully costumed of any on the continent . . . they are all entirely in a state of primitive wildness, and consequently are picturesque and handsome, almost beyond description.'

SOURCE 23
An extract from a letter written by George Catlin in 1832.

SOURCE 24
Poster for 'Buffalo Bill's Wild West Show', 1898.

'Nits breed lice'

The European evidence on pages 12 and 13 was produced by people who were, on the whole, sympathetic admirers of Native American civilisation. Between the 16th and 19th centuries, they were in a minority. Europeans and European-Americans did not understand Native beliefs, customs or lifestyles. They did not think they were important or worth preserving. Many European settlers were openly hostile. One of the most famous 'Indian-haters' was a Dutchman named Tom Quick. He killed many Native American children and was said to have justified these brutal murders with the words 'nits breed lice'. How can hostile evidence like this be used to understand the history of the Native American people?

'I admit that there are good white men, but they bear no proportion to the bad; the bad must be the strongest, for they rule. . . . They enslave those who are not of their colour, although created by the same Great Spirit who created them. . . . There is no faith to be placed in their words. . . . They will say to an Indian, 'My friend; my brother'. They will take him by the hand, and at the same moment, destroy him.'

SOURCE 26
This speech was made by Pachgantshilias, Chief of the Delaware nation in 1787, to an audience of Native Americans and white Christian missionaries.

SOURCE 27
The body of Chief Big Foot, frozen stiff in bitter winter weather, two days after the MASSACRE of the Sioux people at Wounded Knee in 1890.

SOURCE 25
This painting by the European-American artist John Vanderlyn shows the murder in 1777 of a settler, Jane McCrea, by Native warriors who were fighting in the British army.

Cowboys and Indians

The first European settlers arrived in North America during the 16th century. Soon there were frequent fights between Europeans and Native Americans, as settlers moved on to Native American land. Source 25 shows how these clashes were portrayed by Europeans, for a European audience. In contrast, Source 26 gives a Native American view.

By the mid-19th century, these battles had turned into open war. Native Americans fought to defend their lands from ever-increasing numbers of farmers and ranchers and miners seeking gold. These conflicts have left us with some terrible images of suffering and tragedy, such as Source 27. They have also been the subject of countless 'westerns'. These films have created one of the most powerful and misleading images of Native American people as fierce, untrustworthy enemies. You can see a typical 'western' poster in Source 28.

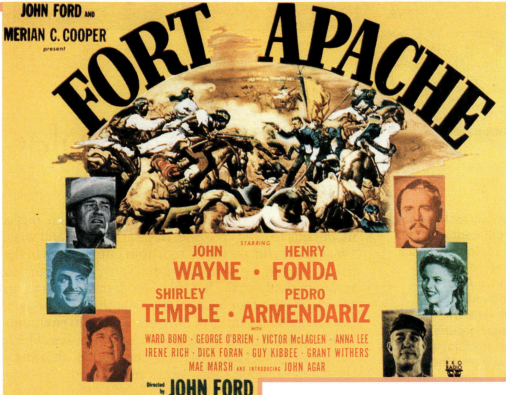

SOURCE 28

A typical Hollywood image of the 'wild west' from 1948.

Stereotypes today

Even if we no longer believe in the 'wild west' version of history, our understanding of the Native American past may still be influenced by present-day concerns. Source 29 tells us about social problems facing some Native American people today. We must be careful to distinguish the present from the past. Just because a group of people is under-privileged today, it does not mean that they have always been weak or hopeless. Source 30, written by a Native American, encourages us to look at American history in a new way. We will try to follow that advice in the rest of this book.

I loved my people so much and missed them if I couldn't see them often. I felt alive when I went to their parties, and I overflowed with happiness when we would all sit down and share a meal, yet . . . the drunken Indians I saw filled me with a blinding hatred. I blamed them for what had happened to me, to the little girl who had died of an overdose of drugs, and for all the girls who were on the city streets. If only they [the men] had fought back, instead of giving up. . . . [But] I realise now that poor people, both white and Native, who are trapped within a certain kind of life, can never look to the business and political leaders of this country for help . . . they'll never change things.

SOURCE 29

An extract from *Halfbreed*, the autobiography of Maria Campbell, the daughter of white and Cree Native American parents living in Canada. Like many 'HALFBREEDS', she faced poverty and discrimination. She wrote her story in 1973.

attainment target 2

1 Look at Sources 25 and 28. Do you think either of these are accurate portrayals of the history of Native Americans? Explain your answer.

2 Are there any sources in this unit which would support the views of American history given in Sources 25 and 28?

3 Westerns, like the one advertised in Source 28, are very popular, even though they may not be accurate history. Why do you think this is? Give two reasons.

'The problem of stereotyping is not so much a racial problem as it is a problem of limited knowledge and perspective [viewpoint]. . . . [To overcome this] ultimately means the creation of a new history . . .'

SOURCE 30

From a book written by the famous Native American spokesman, Vine Deloria Junior (a member of the Sioux nation) in 1970.

Peoples and places

Adapting to the environment

AIMS

In this unit we will look at some of the many different local ENVIRONMENTS of North America. We will look at the different groups of Native American peoples who lived in each environment. Over the centuries, these groups developed ways of living to make the best use of the natural resources all around them.

The North American landscape ranges from high, rugged mountains to deep CANYONS, tropical swamps and wide, open PRAIRIES. Its climate varies, too, from bitter snows in the north to baking heat in the south. How did Native American people manage to survive without the benefit of modern building techniques, farming methods or big machines? On the following six pages, you can see some examples of different American environments, and look at how Native Americans worked out ways of living there. Source 1 provides a key to these case studies, showing you where the different peoples and places can be found.

SOURCE 1

This map shows the natural environments of North America.

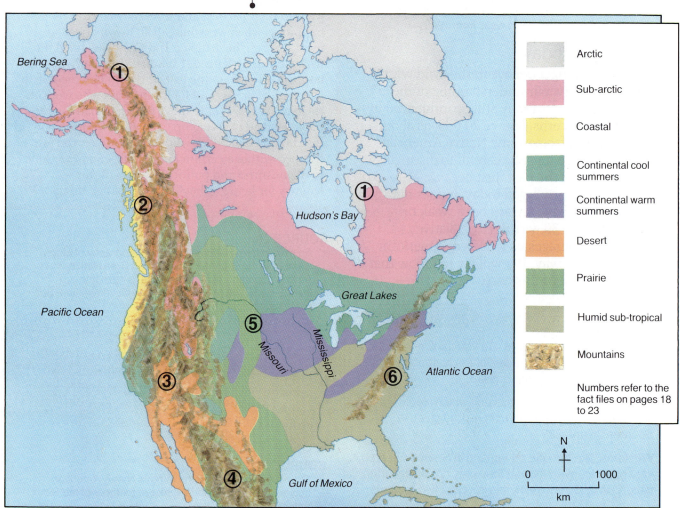

Key:
- Arctic
- Sub-arctic
- Coastal
- Continental cool summers
- Continental warm summers
- Desert
- Prairie
- Humid sub-tropical
- Mountains

Numbers refer to the fact files on pages 18 to 23

> 'The Indian was to a remarkable extent aware of, and sensitive to, his physical environment. He had to be, because the level of his science and technology had not yet got between him and his land.'
>
> 'I could see that the Wasichus [white men] did not care for each other the way our people did. . . . They had forgotten that the earth was their mother.'

SOURCE 2

Two comments about Native American respect for the environment. The first was written by an American historian in 1974 and the second was spoken by a 19th century Native American leader.

SOURCE 3

This illustration, showing Native people digging and planting, comes from a book published in 1591.

American outlook

Native American lifestyles were ancient, and had stood the test of time. (Sadly, none has survived unchanged today.) Case studies show that there was not a single, typical way of life. People in different parts of the continent lived in very different ways. But, as Sources 2 and 3 suggest they all had something in common – a respect for the land. Today, this 'green' outlook is only just beginning to be accepted in the 'developed' parts of the world. Thousands of years ago, Native American people had already recognised that 'the earth is our mother'.

Hunters and gatherers

Everybody needs food, but as you look at the fact files and pictures on pages 18 to 23, you will discover that not all Native American people found food in the same way. Some people were hunters and gatherers. For example, Inuit men went on long, dangerous hunting expeditions. If they managed to kill a whale, it would provide food for their families for several weeks. In winter, the ice and snow formed a ready-made 'deep freeze' for keeping food. In the north-west, men went deep-sea fishing, and helped the women to catch salmon from inland rivers.

People living in the Great Basin looked for food in family groups. They wandered through the desert, searching for seeds, shoots and grubs. They needed expert knowledge of the local wildlife and how the changing seasons affected supplies of food.

Farmers and villagers

Native peoples in other parts of the Americas developed a more settled way of life. They grew crops in the fields that surrounded their homes. During the summer, groups of hunters left these farming villages to chase animals in the woods or prairies. They then returned to the warmth and safety of their homes for the cold winter months.

Almost everyone outside the Arctic and the north-west relied on nuts, seeds, roots and TUBERS to keep alive if the harvest failed, or other stores of food ran low at the end of winter.

Shelter

As well as food, people need shelter. They like to make their houses as warm and comfortable as possible. The design of Native American homes varied. If people lived together in big families, houses were built with room for 30 people or more. For example, Mandan people of the Great Plains area lived in houses large enough for grandparents, parents, aunts and uncles, and all their children. Many houses were built to display their owners' wealth or status. Some Native American houses were very comfortably furnished. By contrast, in poor, harsh environments such as the Great Basin area, people lived in single family groups in small, simple homes made of leaves, twigs and thorns.

SOURCE 4
Thousand Mile Lake and the Klondike Hills in Yukon Alaska.

SOURCE 5
Hunters from the Makah people, Washington State, with a whale they have caught, photographed around 1920.

'A successful whale hunt marks the beginning of a happy year.'

SOURCE 6
This comment about Inuit peoples in the Arctic was written by an American anthropologist in 1977.

SOURCE 7
Members of the Inuit nation building a snow house, around 1913.

FACT FILE 1

NAME OF REGION	Arctic and sub-Arctic.
NATIVE PEOPLES	Inuit, Aleut, Athabascan.
LANDSCAPE	Low, rolling hills.
CLIMATE	Dry, windy and very cold. Ground frozen all year round, sea frozen in winter. No daylight in winter, midnight sun in summer.
WILDLIFE	CARIBOU, wolves, foxes, weasels, LEMMINGS, whales, seals, walrus, fish, ducks, geese, gulls.
VEGETATION	Shrubs, lichens, mosses.
CROPS	None.
WAY OF LIFE	Hunting; struggling to survive in a very harsh environment.
MAIN FOODS	Whale and seal meat and fish. Berries.
HOUSING	Shelters made from blocks of ice or sealskin tents.

SOURCE 8
Reflection Lake and Mount Rainier (4394 metres high), in Washington State.

SOURCE 9
A hook for catching halibut (a kind of fish) made of wood and bone.

FACT FILE 2

NAME OF REGION	North-west coast.
NATIVE PEOPLES	Tlingit, Haida, Nootka, Salish and many others.
LANDSCAPE	Steep, rugged mountains. Rugged coastline, narrow beaches. Fast, deep rivers. Travel difficult on land.
CLIMATE	Mild, wet and foggy.
WILDLIFE	Deer, bears, wolves, otters, beavers, MINK, salmon, herring and other fish, seals and whales.
VEGETATION	Thick CONIFEROUS forests.
CROPS	Edible clover, tobacco.
WAY OF LIFE	Fishing and trapping. As food was plentiful, people lived comfortably.
MAIN FOODS	Salmon: fresh, dried or salted.
HOUSING	Large, sturdy wooden 'halls' shared by many close relatives.

SOURCE 10
This was written by an American historian in 1977.

'The culture was marked by abundance. Caches of food, racked . . . boxed, stored, were present in quantity in every village. The odour of decaying fish and rancid oil lay heavily over each one.'

SOURCE 11
Wooden houses in Bellacoola, on the north-west coast of Canada, photographed around 1900.

1 Native American lifestyles evolved gradually, over thousands of years. The pace of change was slow. From the evidence on these pages, can you suggest reasons for this?

2 Suggest reasons why many Native Americans were cautious about new inventions.

3 Do you follow the same way of life that your parents or grandparents followed? Do you like new inventions?

4 Why do you think the way we live today is so different from the ways of life which Native American peoples followed?

SOURCE 12
Rocky desert landscape, Utah.

SOURCE 13
A woman from the Paiute nation of the Great Basin area, gathering seeds in a basket in 1872.

'The Great Basin . . . is one of the . . . driest and least habitable regions. In some parts of it are low, barren and rocky deserts and large salt flats where human habitation is virtually impossible. Elsewhere, limited water supplies and meagre food resources provided a poor existence for native peoples.'

SOURCE 14
This comment was made by an American historian in 1968.

SOURCE 15
A shelter made of twigs, built in 1873 by members of the Ute nation from Utah.

FACT FILE 3

NAME OF REGION	Great Basin.
NATIVE PEOPLES	Ute, Shoshone, Paiute.
LANDSCAPE	Semi-desert, surrounded by mountains. Canyons and salt lakes.
CLIMATE	Hot very dry summers, bitterly cold winters.
WILDLIFE	Rabbits, rats, locusts, ants, flies, snakes, lizards.
VEGETATION	Bushes and shrubs; pine, juniper and oak trees.
CROPS	None.
WAY OF LIFE	Gathering and some hunting. Population density very low (one person per 80 square kilometres). Ancient, nomadic way of life about 10,000 years old.
MAIN FOODS	Pine-nuts and other seeds, green plant shoots, insects, grubs, rabbits, lizards.
HOUSING	Fragile temporary shelters of grass and branches.

SOURCE 17

Women from New Mexico grinding maize on a stone slab and baking bread in a clay oven in 1892.

SOURCE 16

Acoma Pueblo (village), New Mexico.

'A princely realm . . .'

SOURCE 18

An opinion given by General James Carleton of the United States Army in 1862.

FACT FILE 4

NAME OF REGION	South-west.	**VEGETATION**	Rough grassland. Pine trees on mountains.
NATIVE PEOPLES	Pueblo, Zuni, Hopi, Apache, Navajo and others.	**CROPS**	Maize, beans, pumpkins.
LANDSCAPE	High plateaus, mountains, narrow valleys, rich soils.	**WAY OF LIFE**	Farming using irrigation and some hunting. Sheep-rearing (after Europeans arrived). People lived in close-knit communities.
CLIMATE	Very sunny, with hot, dry summers and cool winters. Occasional heavy storms, but water in short supply.	**MAIN FOODS**	Maize, beans.
WILDLIFE	Deer, antelopes, mountain sheep, rabbits, turkeys.	**HOUSING**	Homes built close together made of sun-dried bricks.

ACTIVITY

1 Work in groups of four, in two pairs. Choose two regions from the fact files on pages 18 to 23. Each pair comes from a Native American nation in one of these regions.

Give a short presentation to the other pair in your group explaining:

- why your homeland is a good place to live in.
- why your homeland is a difficult place to live in.

2 Compare the advantages and disadvantages of living in each homeland.

3 You are a Native American man or woman acting as a guide to travellers. Write a 'survival guide' for them, explaining how to find food and water, and how to make a shelter.

SOURCE 19
Typical Great Plains landscape, Idaho State.

SOURCE 20
Members of the Hidatsa nation chasing buffalo, 1832 to 1833.

SOURCE 21
A tipi belonging to Chief Old Bull of the Sioux nation.

'"The Great American Desert" . . . is almost entirely unfit for cultivation, and of course uninhabitable by a people depending on agriculture for their subsistence [basic needs].'

SOURCE 22
A comment made by Major Stephen Long of the United States Army in 1820.

FACT FILE 5

NAME OF REGION	Great Plains.	**VEGETATION**	Thick, tall grassland and forests in the east. Short grasses, shrubs and cactus in the west. Wild fruit, berries, roots, wild rice.
NATIVE PEOPLES	Cree, Blackfeet, Sioux, Cheyenne, Crow, Mandan, Comanche, Hidatsa, Kansa, Pawnee.		
		CROPS	Maize, beans, squashes, sunflowers, tobacco.
LANDSCAPE	High, rolling plains surrounded by mountains. Wide, fertile river valleys. 'Badland' rocky areas too.	**WAY OF LIFE**	Two different lifestyles: hunters followed buffalo; farmers lived in settled villages but also hunted.
CLIMATE	Bitter winters with heavy snows. Very hot summers (over 40°C in July) with thunderstorms.	**MAIN FOODS**	Buffalo, maize, wild fruits.
		HOUSING	Sturdy earth LODGES (large halls housing about 30 people); buffalo skin TIPIS used on hunting trips.
WILDLIFE	Buffalo herds, antelopes, wolves, deer, COYOTE, GROUSE, hawks, eagles.		

FACT FILE 6

NAME OF REGION	Eastern woodlands.
NATIVE PEOPLES	Natchez, Iroquois, Cherokee and many others.
LANDSCAPE	Marshy coastal plains, low hills rising to mountains.
CLIMATE	High rainfall, warm in south, cool in north.
WILDLIFE	Bears, deer, buffalo, turkeys, fish, turtles.
VEGETATION	Fruit trees, nut trees, berries, root plants.
CROPS	Maize, beans, melons, tobacco.
WAY OF LIFE	Farming plus hunting and gathering. In the colder north of the region hunting was important as fewer crops grew there.
MAIN FOODS	Maize, nuts.
HOUSING	Tipis or 'longhouses' of wooden poles covered with thatch and matting. They had room for several families. Some villages enclosed by a wooden wall.

SOURCE 23
Eastern woodland landscapes range from cold, northern birch forests to this semi-tropical swamp, in Florida.

SOURCE 24
Hunters, disguised in deerskins, drawn by a 16th-century European traveller to America.

SOURCE 25
Tipis made of birchbark by the Ojibwa people of eastern Canada around 1857.

attainment target 3

1 This unit shows the environments where Native Americans lived. How can photographs of the landscape today help us find out about the past?

2 Compare Source 22 with this description of the same territory, written by a 19th-century Native American:
'Crow country is good country. The Great Spirit put it in exactly the right place. Wherever you are in it you fare [do] well. . . . When your horses are fat and strong from the mountain pastures, you can go down on the plains and hunt buffalo.'

a Compare the usefulness and reliability of these two descriptions.
b How can historians use this conflicting evidence?

The old ways

Native nations

As you can see from Source 1, North America was inhabited by many different groups of peoples or nations. Nobody knows for certain how many Native nations there were at the time the Europeans arrived in 1492. Historians have estimated that there may have been approximately 2,000.

Some of these nations, like the Paiute peoples, were divided into smaller groups. Others, like the Iroquois nations of the north-east, formed alliances together. Nations like the Sioux and Comanche of the Great Plains were large and powerful. In contrast, there were many small, isolated communities living in remote areas along the north-west coast.

AIMS

In this unit, we will look at the many different groups, called 'nations', of Native peoples who lived in America before the Europeans arrived. They lived in a way that had developed slowly, over thousands of years. Where did these nations settle? Who were their leaders? How were they organised? What languages did people speak? What did they look like? And what did they believe?

SOURCE 1

Homelands of the largest Native American nations.

What made a nation?

Each nation shared beliefs and traditions. These created a strong sense of identity. People also united against threats from hostile neighbouring nations. But land and language were even more important. Each Native American nation lived and worked in a particular place: they became guardians of that land. All the people belonging to one nation spoke the same language.

There were many different languages in North America. Some scholars have grouped them into 'families' because they developed from the same 'parent' language. However, people from different nations could not usually understand one another, even if they spoke similar languages. Areas like the Great Plains were shared as hunting grounds by several nations. So people living there developed a sign language, which allowed them to communicate in a simple way. Source 2 reveals that this sign language could sometimes lead to confusion.

A sense of history

Native people valued their past (see Source 3). Each nation felt united by its shared history and ANCESTRY. Some nations took great care to record their history. Source 4 shows a painted deerskin made by members of the Kiowa nation. Important events for each year are recorded in picture-writing.

> No Indian knows when our people [the Nez Percés] first reached the Yellowstone River. None know when the first Blackfeet Indians [enemies of the Nez Percés] were met. But Blackfeet is not their proper name, as sign language . . . denotes [shows]. In early days, when meeting different tribes, in talking by signs at a distance telling each other to what tribe they belonged, the Blackfeet always pointed to their leg below their knee, or between the knee and the foot. Their proper name, therefore, is Blacklegs. . . . But the Nez Percé name for these raiders was Iskoikenic [schemers]!

SOURCE 2
Part of a traditional story, from the Nez Percé nation.

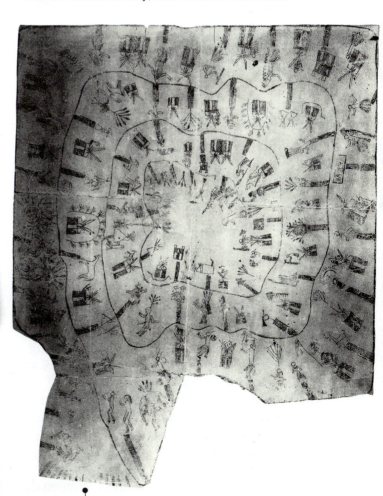

SOURCE 4
A picture-history, from the Kiowa nation. It records important events between 1833 and 1892. The pictures were drawn by Chief Little Mountain and his nephew. The picture-history was consulted so many times that fresh copies had to be made, as the old ones wore out. This is the last surviving copy.

> 'A people without history is like wind on the buffalo grass.'

SOURCE 3
A traditional Sioux saying.

1 Why was its own history so important to each nation?

2 Use these pages to make a list of the factors which might give the British a sense of identity. Which factors are the most important? How important is history as a factor?

SOURCE 5
War leaders from the Mandan nation, meeting to discuss future plans. This painting by George Catlin was made in the 1830s.

Leaders and chiefs

A nation needs some form of government to make important decisions, such as going to war and preventing crime. However, it does not have to have a single leader, like a king or a president. COUNCILS were the most common types of leadership among Native Americans. Members of these councils were men respected for their wisdom and experience. They often came from rich, powerful families.

When the councils met to discuss problems or make plans, women were sometimes allowed to sit close by and shout out their comments. You can read a description of a council meeting, and see a war council in session, in Sources 5 and 6. When a nation went to war, they would choose a wise and brave fighter as their 'chief' (see Source 7). Most nations had several chiefs, all respected in different ways.

It was also possible for leadership to work 'behind the scenes'. Among the Iroquois, the most powerful people were women. Women did not fight, but they owned all the fields and houses. Because they were rich, they controlled the councils. SHAMANS, or magic healers, also held positions of authority in many Native American nations. You can read more about them on page 40.

'Each man was heard with the utmost courtesy for as long as he wished to speak, and each viewpoint was solemnly considered, for the art of persuasion was the essence of such meetings, and each man was entitled to his chance to persuade. No orator [speaker] was interrupted and no council member was permitted to leave the session until . . . [agreement was reached].'

SOURCE 6
A description by a modern European-American historian of traditional council meetings among Native American nations.

SOURCE 7
Mouse-Coloured Feather, a famous warrior from the Mandan people, painted in 1832.

A land without laws?

Early European travellers were puzzled because Native American nations appeared to have no written laws. Laws were not needed: children were taught that they were part of a group. It was everyone's duty to help the group, even if this meant going against their own wishes. Source 8 suggests that this system worked, but it put a lot of pressure on people who disagreed with the views of the group.

People who disobeyed these unwritten rules would be punished. As there were no laws, people could not be put on trial. Instead, they became the victims of gossip, mockery or public disgrace. Sources 9 and 10 explain how this system of punishment worked. Source 11 shows life in a typical Native American community. Group feeling also encouraged people to co-operate in work and leisure. As food supplies were often unpredictable, people were ready to share during times of hardship.

Although co-operation was important within Native American societies, individuals could still be proud and competitive. Some men and women boasted of belonging to a powerful family, or of their wealth and achievements. Within any Native American nation, there were people who were respected for their bravery, skill or wealth. Others who were considered to be lazy or 'odd' were treated with contempt.

> They were a well-disciplined people, maintaining public order under many trying circumstances. And yet . . . there was no code of rules of conduct nor punishment. . . . There were no commandments nor moralising proverbs.

SOURCE 8
This comment was made by a modern Native American anthropologist, looking back at the traditions of his people.

> 'Whenever we departed from the traditions our neighbours would scorn us.'

SOURCE 9
A description of community life around 1900, remembered by a woman from the Hopi people.

1 How was Native American society ruled without written laws? Think of at least two ways.

2 How did Native American systems of government fit in with Native peoples' ways of life?

3 Which do you think is more important in influencing your behaviour – group pressure or written laws?

4 What advantages and disadvantages are there in belonging to a society where you are trained to think of the needs of your group, rather than of your own personal feelings?

> The individual functioned as an individual, but he also functioned as the community. Ridicule and gossip could be directed at him to keep him in line, but he could also be the gossiper when someone else got out of line.

SOURCE 10
A comment made by a modern European-American sociologist.

SOURCE 11
Scene in a Mandan village near St Louis, Missouri. Painted by George Catlin between 1837 and 1839.

SOURCE 12
Chief Tatanka Yotanka (Sitting Bull) of the Sioux nation.

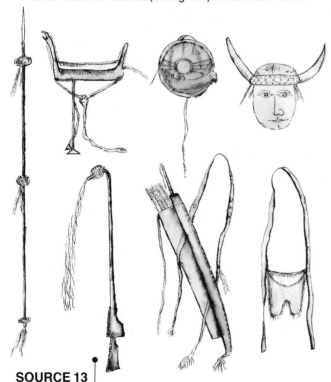

SOURCE 13
Weapons and clothing belonging to a Comanche warrior, sketched by a 19th-century British traveller in Texas: saddle, spear, gun in a case, bow and arrows, bag containing magic charms, head-dress with horns.

Rivals

Why do nations fight? Sometimes they fight to win new lands or to drive out invaders. Sometimes they fight to defend their religious or political beliefs. Some Native American nations, like the Iroquois, used war to win more territory. Other nations battled to keep control of valuable hunting grounds. They also fought to stop other Native peoples settling in their HOMELANDS. Thefts, insults, family squabbles or rivalry among chiefs could all lead to fighting. Source 12 shows a Native American warrior. In Source 13 you can see some weapons that were used by Native Americans.

Pride and daring

The evidence in Source 14, however, suggests a different reason for war. Traditionally, a warrior's pride and daring was as important as his strength. He could demonstrate this by going on surprise RAIDS. Trophies, such as SCALPLOCKS cut from enemies' heads, could be captured and carried home in triumph. (The scalped victims did not always survive.) Touching an enemy with a coup stick – called 'counting coup' – did not harm him at all, although it did damage his reputation. The warrior who counted most coup won even more honour among his comrades than a fighter who killed many enemies. Men from the Great Plains nations wore shirts which were decorated with records of their fighting achievements and showed their rank. Source 15 shows us how one recent American historian has summarised Native nations' attitudes to war.

> **attainment target 1**
>
> 1 Which kind of warfare was most damaging to a nation: raids; battles; counting coup; potlatches? Which was the least damaging? Explain your answers.
>
> 2 Complete this sentence: 'A Native American warrior was respected because. . .'.
>
> 3 Why do you think the Hopi nation called itself the 'Peaceful People'?
>
> 4 Look at Source 16. Now make a list of actions that Native American warriors would have found shameful.

SOURCE 14
Scalp-dance by men of the Minnetaree (Hidatsa) nation, painted by European artist Karl Bodmer in the 1830s.

'Fighting over women, material possessions or hunting rights extended to most . . . of North America. . . . Plunder, adventure and revenge were common causes of warfare . . . participation in warlike activities was mandatory [essential] for any male desiring to be fully accepted into a [Great Plains] tribe.'

SOURCE 15
A comment about Native warfare, made by a modern American historian.

Ta-oya-te-duta [Little Crow] is not a coward, and he is not a fool. When did he run away from his enemies? When did he leave his braves behind him on the warpath and turn back to his tipi? . . . Is Ta-oya-te-duta without scalps? Look at his war feathers. Behold the scalps of his enemies hanging there on his lodge poles.

SOURCE 16
These words were spoken by Chief Ta-oya-te-duta (Little Crow) of the Santee Sioux people in 1862.

'It has been our wish to live here in our country peaceably, and do such things as may be for the welfare and good of our people. . . . When people come to trouble, it is better for both parties to come together without arms and talk it over and find some peaceful way to settle it.'

SOURCE 17
Sinte-Galeshka (Spotted Tail) of the Brulé Sioux people made this speech in 1865.

Peaceful people

It is important to remember that much of our evidence about Native American warriors comes from non-native sources. It was collected at a time when many Native American nations were fighting for their survival.

Source 16 is a brave, defiant statement, made by one Native leader. It reveals warrior values. However, his was not the only voice. Before the Europeans arrived, many Native nations, like the Hopi, prided themselves on being peaceful people. They found non-violent ways of solving conflicts. Among the Pacific coast nations, for example, lavish gift-giving sessions called 'potlatches' were held. These ceremonies demonstrated the giver's wealth and power, winning him or her respect in the community. One historian has called this 'warfare through gifts'. Source 17 tells us that even the Great Plains nations, which had a long tradition of raiding, often preferred settling their quarrels peacefully to avoid war.

Life cycles

Children were welcome in Native American families. New-born babies were greeted with a prayer (Source 18) or with a ritual bath. They were well fed and well cared for, as Source 19 shows. In some nations, such as the Inuit of the Arctic, babies born when food was scarce might reluctantly be killed for the good of the family as a whole. Children born to unmarried mothers might also be put to death, because there was no family to support them. Giving a child a name was usually a sign that it would be allowed to live. In nations where men went hunting, or were involved in constant wars, boy babies were preferred. In nations whose lifestyles centred on women workers, girls were more welcome.

> Sun God, here is our little son Red Arrow. Let your rays fall on him. Give him a healthy body, just as your rays help our crops to grow. Let him grow and become a strong warrior to help defend his people.

SOURCE 18
A traditional prayer from the Navajo people.

SOURCE 20
This painting was made by an Apache artist in the 1890s, using vegetable dyes on deerskin. It shows the ceremony held by Apache peoples to celebrate the time when a girl reaches puberty.

SOURCE 19
An early photograph of a Native American family group from the Bannock (Shoshone) nation. It was taken in Idaho in 1871 by a European-American photographer.

Training for life

As soon as a child was old enough to join in adult work, he or she was expected to learn useful skills. These skills depended on the nation's way of life. Boys learned skills they would need for trapping, whaling, fishing, making and mending weapons, riding and fighting. Girls were taught how to cook, make clothes and look after babies. In farming communities, they also learned how to grow, harvest and store crops. Women taught girls craft skills too: basket weaving, leather work, pottery and embroidery. Fortunately, there was also time for children to play.

When children reached the age of PUBERTY, most nations held special ceremonies to mark their new adult status. Source 20 shows one of these rituals. Puberty was important, as young people were then allowed to marry. Marriages were sometimes arranged; sometimes they took place because a couple fell in love. Source 21 describes courting customs. Usually, arranged marriages meant that a 'bride price' was paid to the girl's father (see Source 22), but the bride's family had to approve the young man's skills and character as well.

Each boy made a four-holed flageolet [like a penny-whistle] . . . to use in serenading. In social dances, the women took the initiative [made the first move] by throwing a small stone or stick into the youth's lap as an invitation to a clandestine [secret] visit to her family camp. These 'girl-hunting' expeditions involved the creeping lover at night in a risky and possibly abruptly-ended courtship, since if he were caught, the girl's family might press for marriage.

SOURCE 21
A modern European-American anthropologist describes the courting customs among the Ute peoples of the Great Basin area.

'Most of the marriages are contracted [arranged] by the parents . . . who are often impatient to be in receipt of the presents they are to receive as the price of their daughters.'

SOURCE 22
A comment made by a 19th-century European-American traveller to the Great Plains.

SOURCE 23
This painting from 1834 shows Comanche women working hard, cleaning and preparing skins for use as clothing.

Men's slaves?

Once couples married, they settled into the roles expected of adult men and women. In most nations, there was a clear distinction between male and female tasks. As we have seen, children were trained for these from an early age. Source 23 shows Great Plains women at work cleaning buffalo skins, while the men lounge at ease. They are probably relaxing now they are safely home after a buffalo hunt. The comment made by Catlin, which you can read in Source 24, may be exaggerated, but on the whole, Native American women did work extremely hard.

Many men married more than one wife. Women did all the domestic work and most of the farming, so a man would enjoy a more

'The Crow women are . . . like all other Indian women, the slaves of their husbands, being obliged to perform all the domestic duties and drudgeries of the tribe.'

SOURCE 24
A comment by the artist and traveller George Catlin, made around 1834.

comfortable home if he had several wives. A man's first wife was usually the most senior woman in the household, but the 'newest' wife was often the favourite. Not all women were happy with these arrangements, but they had little power to change them.

Respect for women

Women earned admiration from men for their artistic achievements and their beauty, as well as for their domestic skills. Source 25, written by a woman, suggests another kind of power. Women were respected for their 'magical' ability to produce children.

The pressure to conform

Today, we are used to people questioning their place in society, and sometimes rebelling against it. In traditional Native American societies, rebellion was normally impossible. People could not survive without the support of their family or their nation, so they had to conform. People who rebelled were outlawed: a terrible punishment which led to a lonely death.

In some Native nations, there were men who were unable to do what society expected. They became pretend women, called 'berdache'. Source 26 describes their lives. Unfortunately, there was no parallel 'escape route' from social pressure for most women.

> You see, we **have** power. Men have to dream to get power from the spirits and they think of everything they can – song and speeches and marching around. . . . But we **have** power. . . . Children. Can any warrior make a child, no matter how brave and wonderful he is?

SOURCE 25
A proud statement made by a woman from the Hopi nation.

> 'Berdache – these were men, some of them homosexuals, who adopted women's clothing and women's roles for life. They were often secondary wives of famous men, and many achieved considerable success as craftsmen in skin tanning, clothing preparation, beadwork and other normally female tasks. The berdache was not an object of ridicule, for he was . . . sacred . . . his role was looked on as . . . perhaps unfortunate, but certainly not of his own doing.'

SOURCE 26
This description was made by a modern European-American anthropologist.

SOURCE 27
Chief Mahpiua-luta (Red Cloud) of the Sioux people, in old age.

Old Age

Native American traditions encouraged respect for old age. Old men and women were valued for the advice they could give, and for the skills they taught younger members of their families, as you can see in Sources 27 and 28. Sometimes, like new-born babies, old people were 'sacrificed' to help the larger family group. Source 29 records the words of a weak, almost blind old man from the Mandan nation who bravely chose to die rather than be a burden to his children as they travelled in search of buffalo. They left him with a little food, beside a small fire, knowing he would soon either starve to death or die from the cold.

'"Respect those old people," mother and father used to say. That is what we used to do.'

'Cheechum (my great-grandmother), my best friend and *confidante*, tried to teach me all she knew about living.'

confidante someone who knows your secrets

SOURCE 28
Two native American women remember the important roles which old people played in their lives when they were young.

I am a burden to my children. . . . I wish to die. Keep your hearts stout, and think not of me; I am no longer good for anything.

SOURCE 29
The sayings of an old man, asking his family to leave him alone to die, written down by George Catlin in the 1830s.

1 Which would you rather have been in Native American society: a woman or a man? Explain your answer.

2 Would you have liked to be a child in a Native American family? List your reasons.

3 Today, role models for men and women are not so clearly fixed as they were in the past. Do you think this is good or bad, for men or for women?

4 In Native American society, new-born babies and frail old people might occasionally be neglected on purpose, so they would die.
  a Why did this happen?
  b What evidence do we have about how Native American people felt about doing this?
  c Why do you think the old man in Source 29 agreed to be left to die?
  d Do you think his choice was made freely?

5 In today's society, do you think killing ill, weak or helpless people can ever be justified? Does it make a difference if the person wants to die? (The text and sources on pages 30 and 31 might also help you.)

Funerals

Funeral customs varied widely among Native nations, but, where possible, people mourned the dead, and treated corpses with honour. Source 30 shows an example of a tree burial. The dead body was left in a tree to decay. Then the bones would be placed in a rocky cave. But sometimes dead bodies were a source of fear. Among the Hopi and Pueblo nations of the south-west, touching a corpse was one of the most awful things you could do. Most people believed in life after death for a person's spirit or soul. A few nations, like the Hopi, believed that spirits returned to haunt living men and women and bring bad luck into the world.

SOURCE 30
This 19th-century photograph shows a tree burial carried out by the Crow people.

Clothes

Clothes keep us warm. They also make a statement about our wealth, status and taste. Clothes tell onlookers whether their wearer is male or female. They also give information about his or her special responsibilities, such as mother, fighter or leader. The style of clothes which Native Americans wore and the fabrics they used depended on the local climate and raw materials. Local traditions were also important; clothes showed what Native nation people belonged to. In the USA today, traditional Native clothes are worn to demonstrate national pride.

SOURCE 31
Mah-to-toh-pah (Chief Four Bears) of the Mandan people, wearing a magnificent war-bonnet and elaborate, fringed buckskin robes. He was painted by Catlin in 1832.

Proud display

Sources 31 and 32 show clothes worn by important men and women among the Great Plains peoples. Source 31 is a portrait of a powerful war leader. His long head-dress is made of eagle feathers; the paintings on his soft BUCKSKIN shirt tell us that he was a successful warrior who had killed many enemies in battle. The buffalo horns and mane worn on his head are a mark of special status. They could only be worn by the very bravest men. The photograph in Source 32 shows the wife of a wealthy man. Her clothes are rich and elaborate, using expensive materials.

SOURCE 32
The wife (we do not know her name) of Spotted Tail of the Brulé Sioux people, photographed in 1872. She is wearing a finely-woven blanket and necklaces of polished teeth and bones.

Patience and skill

These fine clothes took hours of patient work to make, because each garment was carefully sewn and decorated by hand. Like cooking, making clothes was women's work. Skins were carefully stripped from deer which had been killed for food. Then the hair was scraped off, using bone or stone knives. The skins were softened by being rubbed with fat, liver or brains. They were soaked in water, carefully stretched out to dry, and smoothed with wooden polishers. Then they were hung over smoky fires; this helped to keep them soft. Finally, they were cut and sewn, using bone needles and animal SINEWS, to make shirts and leggings for men, or skirts for women.

Ordinary people

The clothes worn by ordinary people were cheaper and simpler. Source 33 shows some examples of 'everyday' shirts, leggings and dresses worn by Great Plains peoples. In the north-west, women wove beautiful blankets from tree bark and goat hair, for the men of their families to wear. You can see one of these in Source 34.

ACTIVITY

North American clothes were carefully made by hand, using natural materials of many different kinds. How would you manage to dress yourself as a Native American? Choose one of the three outfits shown in Sources 31, 32 or 34. Make a list of all the materials which have been used to make and decorate these clothes. If you were trying to make an outfit like this, how would you:
- get the materials you need,
- clean them and prepare them for use,
- assemble them to make your outfit,
- add decorations to give a 'message' about yourself?

SOURCE 33

Children from the Paiute people, in 1873. They are wearing traditional clothes made from buckskin.

SOURCE 34

A wealthy man from the Tsimshian people, from the north-west Canadian coast, photographed in 1885. The faces woven on his coat show his famous ancestors.

Hot and cold

Other everyday clothing styles were developed to meet local needs. In the freezing Arctic regions, people wore fur-lined PARKAS and waterproof MUKLUK BOOTS. You can see examples of these in Source 35. In the Great Basin region, people wore rabbit-skin blankets (see Source 36) to keep warm. In areas where the weather was sunny and mild, people wore very little clothing. Native American people were not offended by nakedness; it seemed sensible in the heat. Source 37 shows a group of men from the south-east, wearing short TUNICS. Among other southern peoples, men wore simple loincloths and women dressed in short aprons.

SOURCE 35
Inuit villagers in traditional bad-weather clothing. Photographed in Alaska before 1887.

SOURCE 36
Members of the Paiute nation wearing rabbit-skin blankets, photographed in 1872.

SOURCE 37
Warriors of the Miami nation, painted by a European artist in 1795. They are wearing simple tunics of lightweight cloth, probably cotton.

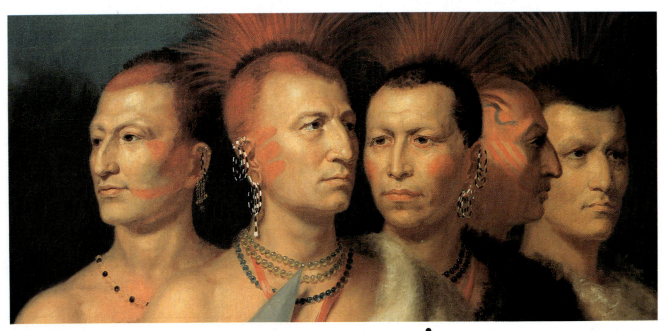

SOURCE 38
A group of leaders from the Pawnee nation, painted on a visit to Washington DC by Charles Bird King in 1821.

Colour and richness

On special occasions, or when they could afford it, Native American men and women liked to wear jewellery and face-paint. Necklaces and earrings made of polished bone were popular; important men often wore grizzly bear claws. In the far north, people also pierced their lips and noses to wear 'labrets' (lip-plugs) and rings. In Source 38, you can see some leaders of the Pawnee people wearing fine jewellery, face paint and elaborate hairstyles.

Fashions in hairdressing varied among different groups of people. Some warriors, like the Pawnee men, shaved their heads using sharp shells and then wore a 'roach' or crest of stiffened animal hair. Others grew their hair long and braided it, or wrapped it in beaver fur. Men plucked out the hair on their faces, as beards and moustaches were not fashionable. Women wore their hair long and loose, or cut to shoulder length with a fringe. Both men and women used fat – bear's grease was best – to keep their hair smooth and shiny.

'After a while, she came back all dressed up and ready. She had . . . a beautifully-coloured hair ornament and she wore many strings of beads around her neck, and bracelets around her wrists. Her fingers were covered with rings and she wore a pair of ornamented leggings. She wore wide-flap ornamented moccasins and in each ear she had about half-a-dozen holes and they were full of small silver pieces made into ear ornaments. She was painted also. She had painted her cheeks red and the parting of her hair red. She was all dressed up.'

SOURCE 39
A description of a bride on her way to her wedding, from around 1900.

Dressing for ceremonies

Source 39 describes a young girl from the Winnebago people, painted and dressed for her wedding. Many women put red paint on their foreheads and in the parting of their hair. Men often painted their bodies before taking part in religious ceremonies. This is probably the origin of the old name for Native Americans – 'Red Indians'. It was given to them by European explorers, who met warriors painted with red-coloured earth. Today, this name is offensive and should not be used.

1 The men shown in Source 38 were all leaders of their nation. How can we tell this from the picture?

2 Source 39 describes a bride dressed for her wedding. Why do people (now and in the past) dress their best for special occasions?

Myths and legends

Each Native American nation had its own language, its own history, and its own set of beliefs. Myths and legends were rooted in the land where a Native nation lived. They often included references to local wildlife, rivers, mountains and trees, as well as to ancient ancestors. They helped people to feel they belonged to their nation and its land. Myths and legends also allowed people to cope with the difficulties and disappointments of life.

The spirit world

All living things had their own spirits. There were also grand, powerful forces which controlled the seasons, the wind and the rain. The Hopi and Navajo called these spirits 'the Holy People' and portrayed them in art and crafts (see Source 40). These spirits normally could not be seen, but they became visible after death or through the use of magic.

SOURCE 40
This design showing 'Holy People', was woven on a rug made by Navajo craft workers.

SOURCE 41
A member of the Blood Native nation of Canada, taking part in the sun dance ritual. This photograph is from 1887.

Offering pain

Any kind of sacrifice pleased the spirits. Sometimes, precious goods were offered: a favourite horse might be given up and set free to roam. Ritual suffering was also used. Mandan people chopped off their fingers; other Great Plains nations held annual dances involving self-torture. Source 41 shows a photograph of a 'sun dance' ceremony. Dancers threaded leather thongs through their flesh, and danced until the skin ripped and they could break free.

Survival strategies

Another kind of ceremony was designed to encourage crops to grow, or rain to fall. Harvest ceremonies gave thanks for good crops, and asked for these blessings to continue in the future. In Source 42, you can read a prayer offered by the Iroquois people at their 'green corn festival'. In the far south-west, the Hopi people made enormous puppets which were larger than life size. These puppets represented the spirits who were believed to bring healthy crops and good fortune to their communities. You can see some of these puppets in Source 43.

> **attainment target 1**
>
> 1 What aspects of Native American life were influenced by religion? Write a sentence on each, showing the part religion played.
>
> 2 Why do you think Native Americans volunteered for ritual torture, like the sun dance (Source 41)?
>
> 3 Did people take part in the white deerskin dance (Source 44) for the same, or for different, reasons?

> Great Spirit in heaven, listen to our words. We have assembled to perform a sacred duty, as thou has commanded. . . . We thank thee for thy great goodness in causing our mother, the earth, to bring forth her fruits. We thank thee that thou has caused Our Supporters [our crops] to yield abundantly. . . . Preserve us from all danger. Preserve our aged men. Preserve our mothers. Preserve our warriors. Preserve our children. We burn this tobacco; may its smoke arise to thee.

SOURCE 42

A traditional Iroquois prayer, which was first written down in the 19th century.

Wealth and power

Ceremonies were social as well as religious events. People who took part felt closer together. Sometimes whole communities joined in, sometimes just a small group. The 'white deerskin dance' of the Hupa nation from California allowed rich people to display their wealth and give thanks for it (Source 44). Certain rituals, for example, the riotous 'mask dance' of the Inuit people, provided an excuse for people taking part to break free from normal patterns of behaviour. You can see a mask used for the creation myth dance in Source 45.

SOURCE 43

Giant puppets, representing rain gods, taking part in a house-blessing ceremony at Zuni Pueblo, New Mexico. This photograph was taken around 1897.

SOURCE 45

A mask representing an eagle ancestor, worn by members of the Bella Coola nation during their creation myth dances. Made before 1913.

SOURCE 44

Dancers from the Hupa people of northern California, photographed around 1890. They are ready to begin the white deerskin dance.

attainment target 1

1 Why do you think the mask dancers wore masks (Source 45) when they danced and played tricks?

2 Do you think that Native American people were afraid of them, and of the figures in Source 43, even though they knew it was their friends and neighbours dancing?

Free from harm

Sometimes, ceremonies and sacrifices were not enough to protect people from harm. If people became seriously ill, Native Americans sought professional help from a shaman, or spirit healer. Shamans existed in almost all Native American communities, see Sources 46 and 47. Shamans were usually men, but women past childbearing age could also perform this role.

Healing rituals

Native Americans had expert knowledge of medicinal plants, and knew how to treat simple accidents and injuries. Shamans were called when these straightforward remedies failed. They tried to cure patients with help from the spirits. To the sound of chanting and the rhythmic beat of drums, shamans fell into a TRANCE, uttered strange cries, trembled, drooled, twitched and rolled on the ground (see Source 46). The shamans claimed that while they were in a trance, their souls left their bodies and entered the spirit world. Shamans were powerful people within Native American communities, as Source 48 explains. They were often wealthy, since they charged high fees for their healing powers. Although shamans played an important part in many nations, they were always outsiders. Some shamans had genuine religious beliefs; others were misfits or people with problems. A fair number were tricksters, who fooled weak people or even blackmailed them.

SOURCE 46
A shaman (in costume) treating a sick child, while the child's father beats a drum. Photographed in Kitwanga, British Columbia, 1910.

SOURCE 47
Mah-tohe-ha (Old Bear), a shaman from the Mandan people, painted by George Catlin in 1834.

Soul loss

Why did people hope shamans could help them? Beliefs varied among nations, but many Native Americans thought that illness was caused by 'soul loss', and that a person could be cured if a shaman lured their soul back into their body.

Native Americans also believed that they could become ill if an invisible 'evil object' entered their bodies. This evil object might have been 'sent' by an enemy, or it might have crept in if the sick person had eaten a forbidden or TABOO food or if they had ignored a special custom. From a modern, scientific point of view, these explanations do not make sense. But shamans' cures sometimes worked, especially if the patient's illness was caused by stress or tiredness, or by mental-health problems. Doctors today think that faith and hope (which shamans encouraged) really can help people recover.

> In councils of war and peace, they . . . are regularly consulted before any public step is taken, and the greatest deference and respect is paid to their opinions.

SOURCE 48
A description of the respect paid to shamans, from George Catlin's account of his travels in the 1830s.

1 Why do you think shamans were so powerful? Why were they feared? Why did they become rich?

2 Dancing, speaking in strange 'tongues', or falling into a trance have been part of religious experience for people of different faiths in many parts of the world. Why do you think this has happened?

3 Do you think we respect doctors more than priests in our culture today? If so, why?

Pictures in the sand

There were other ways of using religion to try and heal sick people. The Navajo nation made 'dry paintings' (sometimes called sand paintings) in fields or indoors on the floor. You can see an example in Source 49. These SACRED pictures were part of a long, complicated ritual, with prayers and songs, designed to restore harmony to the community, and make people better. They portrayed the great spirits who ruled the world. The patient would sit on the picture, close to the spirits, and drink a herbal medicine. After the ceremony, the painting would be destroyed.

SOURCE 49
This sand painting was made by Navajo people in Arizona. It shows Mother Earth and Father Sky watching over the universe.

Contact and change

Old and new

When the first Europeans arrived in America, Native lifestyles were thousands of years old. Native communities were proud of their traditions and did not want to alter them. Of course, there were changes: in craft techniques, clothing styles and even systems of political organisation, but they happened slowly and gradually. After the Europeans arrived, the pace of change increased, as Europeans brought new ideas and new technologies with them. Most Europeans did not set out to destroy Native traditions. But sadly, through their ignorance and greed, that was what happened.

Traditionally, very few Native nations were self-sufficient. They needed to trade their own produce for crops and craft goods from elsewhere. Source 1 shows two ancient trade networks, and the goods and raw materials that were traded.

AIMS

In this unit, we will look at early contacts between Native American peoples and European 'new arrivals' in America, from AD 1492 onwards. We will consider the impact of European trade and technology on traditional Native American life. We shall see what Native peoples gained, and lost, from the Europeans living in their land.

SOURCE 1

Two of the most important areas of trade among Native American nations in the centuries before Europeans arrived.

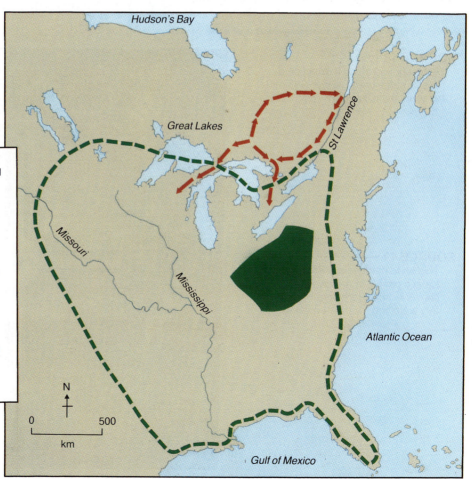

Centre of the Adena-Hopewell civilisation

The Adena-Hopewell trading area which flourished from around 700 BC to AD 1000. Goods traded included semi-precious stones, lead, crystal, shells, silver, pottery and fish

Trade routes operated by the Huron people in the 15th and 16th centuries. They traded in furs and other woodland produce

European trade

Europeans in America soon realised that this 'new found land' could yield rich profits. Customers back home were eager to buy American products, especially furs and tobacco. European merchants formed trading companies, like the Hudson's Bay Company which was founded in 1670. There were also independent ADVENTURERS from the Netherlands and France, who traded with Native peoples in the northern woodlands of America (see Source 2).

European trade did not help Native nations. Items such as iron knives, cooking pots and blankets were exchanged for Native products. However, they were poor quality replacements for the traditional Native-made goods. Many Native people became trapped in debt to European traders. They were forced to leave their homes and work as servants in colonial towns. Trade also damaged Native culture. European-made glass beads replaced beautiful QUILL WORK traditionally produced by Native women, as you can see from Source 3.

SOURCE 2
French fur-trappers, from an engraving by a 19th-century European artist.

1 Some changes in traditional Native American society were the result of deliberate European policy, some were the result of Europeans' thoughtlessness and ignorance. Give an example of each.

2 Should the Europeans be blamed for all their actions which damaged Native American society? Should they only be blamed for damage which was deliberate? Explain your answer.

SOURCE 3
A box decorated with quill work made by women from the Micmac nation and a European-style hood decorated with beads by women from the Chippewa nation.

'I have seen two generations of my people die. Not a man of the two generations is alive now but myself.'

'Englishman, take that land, for none is left to occupy it.'

SOURCE 4
Comments made by two 16th-century Native American leaders: Chief Wahunsonacock of the Powhatan nation and Chief Massasoit of the Wampanoag nation.

Drunkenness and disease

The trade in whisky and rum caused even more damage. Alcohol destroyed Native lives. Native nations were not used to drinking alcohol or coping with the effects of alcohol addiction. European traders knew this, and encouraged their Native trading partners to get drunk so they would become weak and confused.

Worse still, Native American peoples had no defences against European disease. Millions died from measles, smallpox and sexually-transmitted diseases which they caught from European traders (Source 4). Some historians think these diseases may have been deliberately spread by a few European traders to 'clear' Native land for new European homes.

Horses and guns

For thousands of years, many parts of the vast Great Plains area of North America were uninhabited. People lived only in the river valleys where the land was good for farming. In summer, they set off (on foot) across the wide plains grasslands, chasing herds of deer and buffalo. In winter, they returned to the safety of their village homes.

After the Europeans arrived, this traditional way of life changed. More and more Native peoples moved to make their home out on the open plains. Why did this happen? It was partly because Native peoples needed new territory after European settlers drove them out of their traditional homelands. They moved westwards into the 'empty' plains to escape the Europeans, or other Native nations facing similar pressure from settlers.

SOURCE 5

Comanche horsemen practising battle skills, painted by eye-witness George Catlin in the 1830s.

1 Many Native American religious ceremonies among people living on the Great Plains were connected with buffalo hunting. Can you explain why?

2 Horses changed some Native American people's lives completely. Can you think of one or two modern inventions that have revolutionised people's lives today? Give reasons for your answer.

Horses

This changed lifestyle was made possible because, for the first time ever, Native American people had horses. In the 16th century, Spanish settlers in Mexico brought horses and donkeys with them. By around 1700, many Native Americans had stolen or bought these 'new' animals for their own use. Occasionally, horses escaped and roamed freely on the plains. Over the years, large herds of wild horses grew up; young foals could be captured and trained, and were highly prized, see Source 5.

On the move

Horses, donkeys and MULES caused a transport revolution. Native American peoples could now travel much further, and much faster. On horseback, hunters could chase and keep up with the herds of deer and buffalo on the Great Plains. They no longer had to stay within a few days' walking distance of their homes.

Before they had horses, it was difficult for Native American people to transport heavy loads. Ferrying goods by boat was best if there was a suitable river close by. Otherwise, loads had to be carried by people (often women) or by dogs. Source 6 shows a traditional dog travois. This was a kind of sledge, made of wooden poles. Horses could carry much heavier burdens than women or dogs, and this made it possible for people on the plains to develop a nomadic lifestyle. They spent all year travelling, and relied on buffalo for food, shelter, clothing and many other needs, as you can see from Source 7.

SOURCE 6

Bull's Head of the Nez Percé nation, with his wife and a dog-pulled travois.

SOURCE 7

Great Plains peoples used every part of the buffalo they killed. Some historians estimate that there were over 70 different items made from buffalo meat, bones, sinews and skin.

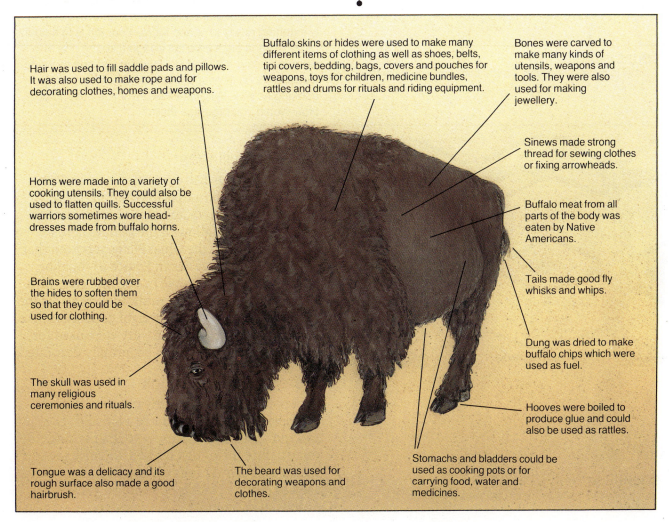

Hair was used to fill saddle pads and pillows. It was also used to make rope and for decorating clothes, homes and weapons.

Buffalo skins or hides were used to make many different items of clothing as well as shoes, belts, tipi covers, bedding, bags, covers and pouches for weapons, toys for children, medicine bundles, rattles and drums for rituals and riding equipment.

Bones were carved to make many kinds of utensils, weapons and tools. They were also used for making jewellery.

Sinews made strong thread for sewing clothes or fixing arrowheads.

Horns were made into a variety of cooking utensils. They could also be used to flatten quills. Successful warriors sometimes wore head-dresses made from buffalo horns.

Buffalo meat from all parts of the body was eaten by Native Americans.

Brains were rubbed over the hides to soften them so that they could be used for clothing.

Tails made good fly whisks and whips.

Dung was dried to make buffalo chips which were used as fuel.

The skull was used in many religious ceremonies and rituals.

Hooves were boiled to produce glue and could also be used as rattles.

Tongue was a delicacy and its rough surface also made a good hairbrush.

The beard was used for decorating weapons and clothes.

Stomachs and bladders could be used as cooking pots or for carrying food, water and medicines.

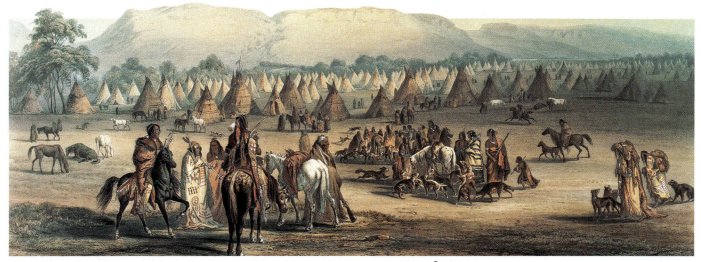

SOURCE 8
A tipi encampment on the Great Plains, painted by George Catlin in 1834.

> Cut thin slices of fresh buffalo meat and hang them to dry in a warm breeze. Protect them from rain. When they are completely dry and hard, pound them (using stones) until you get a fine meat powder, like sawdust. Mix carefully with melted buffalo fat and flavour with dried berries. Pack into buffalo skin bags or buffalo bladders, and store in a cool, dry place.

SOURCE 9
How to make pemmican. Do you think you would like to eat it?

ACTIVITY

You are a Native American woman living on the Great Plains. A herd of buffalo has been sighted. Hunters are getting ready to chase them. Your job is to help the other women pack up a tipi village (like the one in Source 8), to get it ready to move in just one morning. You have to fit in your usual tasks of childcare and cooking as well. What are the tasks you need to do? How would you organise them?

Travelling villages

Nomadic families had no settled homes. They lived in buffalo-skin tipis (like tents). These could be taken down and moved from place to place as hunters followed the buffalo herds. Early travellers to the Great Plains reported that an entire tipi 'village' (as in Source 8) could be packed up, ready to move in one morning. Rich, long-lasting foods like pemmican were made for journeys (Source 9). Lightweight containers, like the parfleche (bag) in Source 10, were used for travelling: they were often beautifully decorated.

Warriors on horseback

Horses were also a great advantage in warfare. Warriors, like those in Source 11, could stage 'hit and run' attacks on enemy settlements, and ride away before their enemies had a chance to fight back. As Source 12 tells us, horses soon became used as proud symbols, identifying Native American nations.

SOURCE 10
A parfleche made by Sioux craft workers from South Dakota.

See them prancing.
They come neighing,
They come a Horse Nation.
See them prancing.
They come neighing,
They come.

SOURCE 12
A war-song used by Great Plains warriors. It was first written down in the 19th century.

SOURCE 11
Great Plains warriors drawn by Howling Wolf of the Cheyenne people in 1876.

Knives and guns

Traditionally, Native American peoples fought with spears, clubs, bows and arrows. European traders introduced new technology into Native warfare (see Source 13). Imported iron knife-blades, fixed to wooden clubs, could cause horrific injuries. Guns, gunpowder and bullets were all bought at a high price from European traders. These new weapons gave the Native nations who owned them tremendous power over the peoples who did not.

Source 14 tells us how Native peoples who lived close to European settlements along the east coast of North America soon became involved in the settlers' wars. Their fighting skills, using both new and traditional weapons, were admired. But however skilfully they fought, Native peoples always ended up the losers. By helping one European army to defeat another, they were also helping to strengthen a fighting force that might, one day, be turned against them.

SOURCE 13
Warriors from the Ute nation holding guns. They were photographed in 1874.

attainment target 1

1 In what ways did horses change Native American lifestyles? In what ways did guns change them?

2 Which aspects of Native American lifestyles were not changed by horses or guns?

3 Explain the difference between the ways guns changed the lives of Native Americans at first, and in the long term.

4 Do you think the movement of Native Americans on to the Great Plains was a change for the better or for the worse? Explain your answer.

During the many conflicts, they were often willing players, choosing sides based on what they considered to be their best interests in protecting their territories, maintaining trade, or settling old inter-tribal scores. Moreover, they often fought on one side or another for what the whites offered them – bounties for scalps, regular pay and rations, firearms and blankets. And, as allies at war, the Indians were worth any price.

SOURCE 14
This comment was made by a modern European-American historian.

A new image?

The earliest contacts between Native American peoples and European settlers brought changes to the way in which Native nations were led. Native chiefs were used to leading their nations in peace as well as in war. After the arrival of the Europeans, Native leaders had to spend most of their energy trying to defend their nations. There was little time to make plans for peace, or for future welfare.

Most Native American peoples chose to fight against the newcomers, rather than to give up their lands. A new type of leader (like Chief Standing Bear, shown in Source 15) emerged to guide them. These leaders were very intelligent and courageous. They were skilful politicians and diplomats, as well as warriors.

In Source 15, Chief Standing Bear is shown clutching a deadly weapon. But in real life, he preferred to use peaceful methods of defence. He took the US government to court to force them to grant civil rights to his nation. Standing Bear won his case, but government officials illegally ignored the court ruling. So many Native American people still lost their rights to land.

attainment target 2

Source 15 gives an heroic, glamorous image of Chief Standing Bear. He is shown as a proud, dignified figure, standing alone.

1 What image of Native American leaders is the photographer trying to portray in Source 15?

2 From what you know about Native American leaders, do you think that this is an accurate image? (Pages 24 to 29 might help you here.)

3 How does Source 15 suggest that Native American ways of leadership might have changed?

In fact, Native American leadership had not really changed. What had happened was the invention of photography. Admiring portraits were made by European and American photographers which gave a romantic image of Native American leaders.

4 Why did photographers portray Native American leaders in this way?

5 Which image of Native American leaders do you think is more accurate, Source 15 or Source 20?

SOURCE 15
Chief Standing Bear, photographed around 1880.

SOURCE 16
Leaders of the Cheyenne and Kiowa nations, photographed with US politicians' wives at the White House in 1863.

'I want to make a big treaty. . . . I will keep my word until the stones melt. . . . God made the white man and God made the Apache, and the Apache has just as much right to the country as the white man. I want to make a treaty that will last, so that both can travel over the country and have no trouble.'

SOURCE 17
Spoken by Chief Delshay of the Apache nation, 1871.

SOURCE 18
Goyathlay (Geronimo) who led the Apache nation against US government troops, photographed in 1884.

SOURCE 20
Little Six, a leader of the Sioux nation, photographed in prison in 1865.

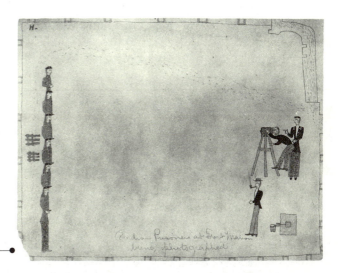

SOURCE 19
A drawing made by a Native American prisoner in 1875, showing prisoners being photographed by European-Americans.

Government deceit

European settlers, and later the United States government, feared the power of Native leaders. They tried to destroy traditional leadership by encouraging disagreements among Native American nations. They offered bribes to leaders whom they hoped would become their friends. Source 16 shows a group of powerful men from Native nations who had been invited to the government headquarters in Washington DC. Source 17 gives an example of how some Native American leaders chose to try and make friendly TREATIES with settlers and the government.

False friendship

Native people found that offers of friendship could not be trusted. A few years after the photograph in Source 16 was taken, three of the four Native leaders at the front of the photograph had been killed by troops who had come to take over their land. Many chiefs, like Geronimo in Source 18, stayed loyal to their people and led them to fight against the Europeans. These chiefs were hunted like criminals by Europeans. If they were caught they were imprisoned or even killed. Source 19 shows a drawing made by a Native artist in a government prison. The government photographer is recording shameful images like the one in Source 20.

Spirit power

In unit 3, we saw that religious beliefs were very important to Native American people. Men and women tried to get closer to the spirits through dreams, fasting, dancing, VIGILS and ritual purifying baths. When people started a difficult task or journey, they would seek guidance from the spirits (see Source 21). Some families believed that they could receive spirit power by communicating directly with wild animals, as you can see from Source 22.

Under attack

After the Europeans arrived, Native American beliefs were under attack. Settlers and traders were hostile to Native religious ideas. Christian MISSIONARIES did not understand how closely Native American beliefs were linked to traditional ways of life. Some Europeans regarded Native people as 'savages', and thought their beliefs were evil. Source 23 reveals some insensitive European attitudes towards Native American beliefs.

> 'Once I was digging roots . . . and I got very tired. I made a pile of earth with my digging stick, put my head on it and lay down. In front of me there was a hole in the earth made by the rains, and there hung a grey spider, going up and down, up and down on its long thread. I began to go to sleep and I said to it: "Won't you fall?" Then the spider sang to me.'

SOURCE 22
The experience of a woman from the Hopi people, round about 1900.

> We do not want to interfere with your religion, but you must talk about practicable things. Twenty times over, you repeat that the earth is your mother. . . . Let us hear it no more, but come to the business at once.

SOURCE 23
This comment was made by United States Army General O.O. Howard, during negotiations with Nez Percé leaders in 1877.

> One of the Bear people felt grieved and went out into the wilderness to fast. His desire was to be blessed by the spirits who are in control of war. . . . Soon he heard someone saying 'Do not cry any more, we have come after you from above. The spirits have blessed you. With victory on the warpath do we bless you.'

SOURCE 21
A traditional story told by the Winnebago people.

1 How did religion help Native Americans to fight against people trying to take over their land?

2 Why do you think ghost dancers believed in the power of holy shirts to protect them?

3 In the USA and many other countries today, people (especially soldiers) swear loyalty to their nation's flag. Can you explain why symbols like flags are important? Do you think Native American symbols, like medicine bundles and totems, were important in the same way?

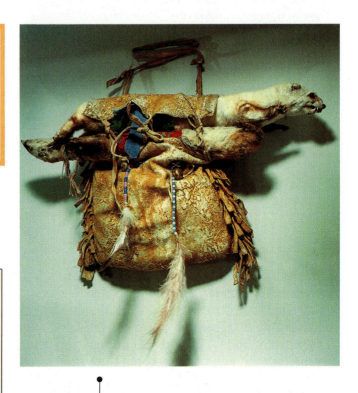

SOURCE 24
A medicine bundle from the Crow Nation. Medicine bundles are sacred objects. Today some Native Americans feel that medicine bundles should not be photographed. Do you agree with this view?

Native beliefs

Native American beliefs were very strong. They lasted long after missionaries and settlers first reached America. For over 200 years after the Europeans arrived, warriors still carried magical painted shields with them when they went into battle. They also continued to keep MEDICINE BUNDLES and sacred IDOLS which you can see in Sources 24 and 25.

Two important Native religious movements grew up after the arrival of the Europeans, at a time when Native nations seemed to be facing certain defeat. The 'Ghost Dance' movement (Source 26) was inspired by a member of the Paiute nation called Wovoka. He taught people to lead pure, peaceful lives and to prepare for the end of the world. His followers believed that soon the ghosts of Native peoples' ancestors would return to live on earth. In this beautiful new world, the old ways of life would be restored and Native American people would once more enjoy freedom and dignity in their own land.

Ghost dancers fell into trances and had amazing 'waking dreams'. They wore holy shirts which they believed would protect them from bullets. Tragically, they were proved wrong. The Ghost Dance movement declined after many of its followers were massacred by US troops in 1890 at Wounded Knee.

SOURCE 26
Ghost dancers from the Arapaho nation, photographed in 1891.

SOURCE 25
A replica (museum-made copy) of a sacred idol belonging to the Kiowa nation. It is made of stone, eagle feathers and deerskin. The original was used in important religious ceremonies.

SOURCE 27
Peyote Way worshippers (sheltering in a tipi) sharing food after all-night prayers. This photograph was taken in 1892.

Peyote Way

The second new Native religion is known as the 'Peyote Way'. Followers of the Peyote Way held meetings for worship where they ate morsels of a fungus, called peyote (see Source 27). Worshippers who had eaten the peyote had dramatic visions which helped them feel closer to God. Followers of the Peyote Way shared their visions and prayers and ate special meals together. This helped them to feel united. In 1918 they formed the Native American Church which still has many members today.

Whose America?

Contact and conflict

The history of meetings between European and Native American peoples is not a happy one. All too often, contact led to conflict. The first recorded fighting between Native peoples and new arrivals took place shortly after AD 1000. Some Viking adventurers, led by Lief Erikson, clashed with Native people living on the Canadian coast – probably members of the Beothuk nation. After a few years, the Vikings sailed away. They found the land too cold and barren.

After Columbus's historic voyage of 1492, travellers and explorers hurried to what they called this 'New Found Land'. Europeans who travelled to the Americas in the 16th and 17th centuries regarded Native American people like friendly children, or like wild animals which could easily be tamed. At first, they were not seen as a threat. In return, many Native American leaders realised it was more comfortable to live peacefully alongside the Europeans rather than to fight, as you can see from Sources 1 and 2. But many people did not agree. There were massacres and atrocities by settlers and by Native American warriors.

AIMS

In this unit, we will look at the fighting that took place in North America after foreign settlers arrived. We will see why it broke out and whether anything could have prevented it happening. We end by finding out how Native American civilisations have managed to survive until today.

SOURCE 1

English settlers in eastern America sign a treaty with local Native American leaders in 1681. From a 19th-century painting by a European-American artist.

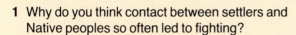

1 Why do you think contact between settlers and Native peoples so often led to fighting?

2 Do you think Powhatan's attitude (Source 2) towards the European settlers was wise? Remember that we have the benefit of knowing what happened in the years after Powhatan's death. Try to answer this question:
 a from Powhatan's point of view, and then
 b from the point of view of a modern historian, looking back.

'I am not so simple as not to know it is better to eat good meat, sleep comfortably, live quietly with my women and children, laugh and be merry with the English, and, being their friend, trade for their copper and hatchets, than to run away from them. … Take away your guns and swords, the cause of all our jealousy, or you may die in the same manner.'

SOURCE 2
Part of a speech made by Chief Powhatan at a meeting for white settlers and Native peoples in Virginia in 1609.

At gunpoint

At first, the number of settlers was small compared with the total Native American population. There was room for both peoples to live in peace. But as more and more settlers arrived throughout the 17th and 18th centuries, these 'new' European-Americans wanted Native territory.

Settlers and soldiers made treaties (like the one shown in Source 1) with some Native American leaders, in order to gain land. Other leaders, like King Philip of the Wampanoag nation, remained strongly opposed to handing over Native land. However, the Europeans were well armed and determined. Even though many Native people resisted, in the end they had no choice. Native peoples also became caught up in fighting between rival groups of settlers, especially the English, French and Dutch. You can see the early wars between 'new' European-Americans and Native Americans in Source 3.

SOURCE 3
Wars between Native Americans and settlers, 1601 to 1845.

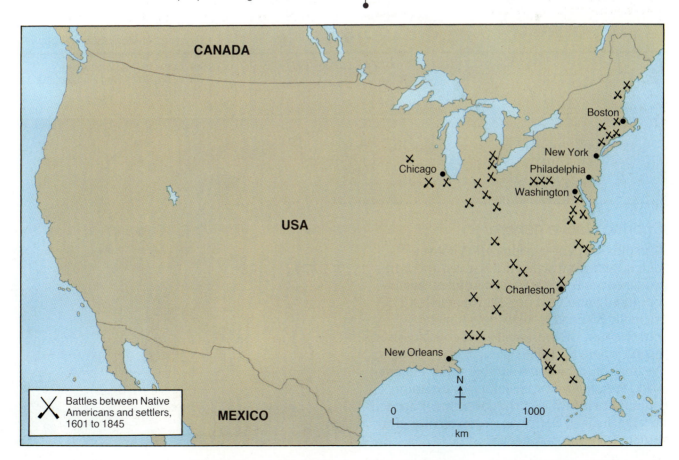

Battles between Native Americans and settlers, 1601 to 1845

Wars for the west

By 1803, the number of 'new' or non-Native Americans totalled four million. Many of them lived in a narrow strip of land along the eastern coast or around the Great Lakes in Canada. These areas were now becoming crowded. There were constant calls to expand this new European-American settlement westwards, towards the 'unknown' heart of the continent. Of course, the land was only 'unknown' or empty from the easterners' point of view; it had been the home of Native peoples for centuries. European-Americans were also becoming better organised. In 1783, the United States of America was formed, after a group of 13 colonies rebelled against British rule. The European-American people had become an independent nation.

> The exodus of this whole people from the land of their fathers is not only an interesting but a touching sight ... they have defended their mountains and their stupendous canyons with a heroism that any people might be proud to emulate [copy]; but when, at length, they found it was their destiny . . . to give way to the insatiable [hungry and greedy] progress of our race, they threw down their arms [weapons].

SOURCE 4
These words were spoken by US General Carleton in 1864. He was describing the removal of the Navajo people from their homeland by the US Army.

SOURCE 5
The overland trails which settlers followed westwards in the 19th century.

SOURCE 6
Fighting between US Army troops and Native American warriors at the battle of Little Bighorn in 1876, drawn by Red Horse of the Sioux nation.

[Map with legend: ••••• Overland trails between 1830 and 1870. Labels: Missouri, OREGON, Oregon Trail, California Trail, Great Salt Lake, Mormon Trail, UTAH, COLORADO, San Francisco, CALIFORNIA, Old Spanish Trail, Santa Fe Trail, Dodge City, St Louis, TEXAS. Scale: 0 — 1000 km. N compass.]

Ignoring Native rights

Who did this nation belong to? Who were its leaders, and what rights did Native American people have? The first US governments were composed entirely of non-Native peoples. They originally planned to allow only limited settlement in the west, and to reserve large areas of land where Native peoples could continue to live in traditional ways. But this policy did not work. Pressure from the European-American community meant that the government opened up large areas of Native American territory for settlers from the east.

'Manifest Destiny'

A powerful idea, called 'Manifest Destiny', developed to support this change in policy. It claimed that Native American civilisation had reached the end of its natural life, and that a European-American civilisation was 'destined' (designed) to take its place. It was all part of God's plan. You can see how one US Army leader explained this view in Source 4. People were encouraged to move westwards by such ideas; they were also attracted by cheap land and the chance to make their fortunes. The routes which people used to travel westwards are shown in Source 5.

From the Native American viewpoint, these new settlers were invading and spoiling their home. The OVERLAND TRAILS ran right across traditional hunting grounds, scaring animals away. The settlers threatened sacred Native sites with their mines and railway tracks.

Not surprisingly, bitter fighting broke out, with many casualties on both sides (Source 6). European-style images portrayed Native Americans as vicious savages, but Source 7 gives a Native American point of view, blaming the settlers for the fighting. You can see a summary of the 'wars for the west' in Source 8.

1 Why do you think the US government gave political rights only to white settlers and their descendants?

2 Do you think that the policy of setting up reservations for Native Americans was fair?

3 Was the government's reservation policy doomed to failure from the start?

4 Why was the idea of 'Manifest Destiny' so popular?

5 Why did white settlers risk great dangers and hardships to migrate to the west?

6 Who was to blame for 'the wars for the west'?

'When the white man comes into my country, he leaves a trail of blood behind him.'

SOURCE 7
These words were spoken by Mahpiua-luta (Red Cloud) of the Sioux nation, in 1865.

SOURCE 8
The 'wars for the west', 1846 to 1890.

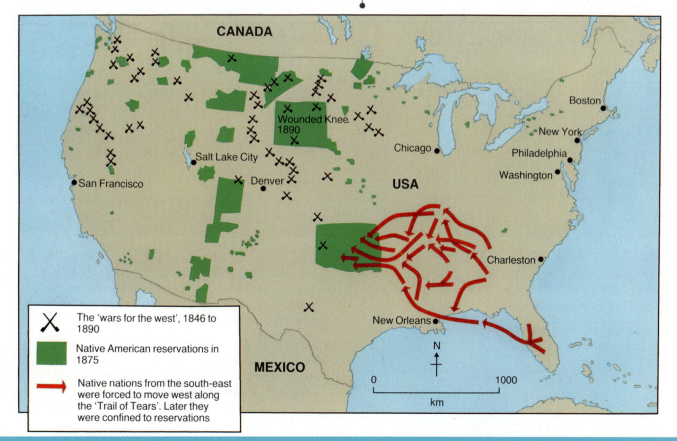

	The 'wars for the west', 1846 to 1890
	Native American reservations in 1875
	Native nations from the south-east were forced to move west along the 'Trail of Tears'. Later they were confined to reservations

SOURCE 9
From a painting by the European-American artist, John Gast, made in 1872.

SOURCE 10
A heap of 40,000 buffalo hides waiting to be loaded on to railway wagons in Dodge City, Kansas, in 1874.

The end?

Source 9 shows how new Americans liked to view their achievements. During the 19th century, they brought 'progress' – roads, railways, electricity, industry, mechanised farming, education and the Christian faith – to the 'wild' west. But look at the left hand side of the picture. The Native American people are shown running away, weak and frightened. There was no place for them, it seemed, in the modern world.

The railways allowed new settlers to travel to all parts of the USA quickly and cheaply; they also threatened Native American lives. Source 10 shows an enormous heap of buffalo skins from animals shot on the Great Plains. They are waiting to be transported by rail to leather factories in the east. Hunters killed so much wildlife, and farmers fenced off so much land, that by the end of the 19th century, buffalo were almost extinct. As a result, many Native American people were starving.

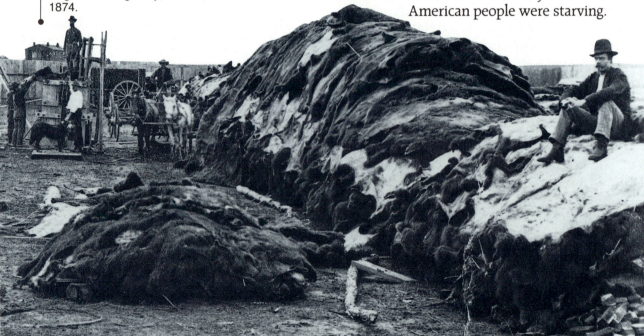

1 Look at Source 9 and at the image it portrays of 19th-century America. How much of this image is fact, and how much opinion?

2 How many different symbols of 'progress' can you see in Source 9?

3 Do all these symbols still mean progress today?

4 What message do you think Source 9 gave to the people who looked at it? Do you think the message was the same for Native Americans as for European-Americans?

5 Now look at Source 10. It is another very powerful image. What message do you think it gave to Native Americans and to European-Americans? What message does it give to us today?

SOURCE 11
Apache families queuing for food rations on an Arizona reservation in 1899.

THE MUSEUM OF MODERN ART, NEW YORK

SOURCE 12
Pupils in a European-style school studying American history, around 1899. Even though the Native American who stands in front of them is alive, they are being taught about Native American civilisation as if it were dead and gone.

❝ [I saw] specimens of worked muslin [fine cotton], and other needlework . . . all proving clearly that [Indians] are capable of civilisation. ❞

SOURCE 13
The opinion of an Englishwoman, Frances Trollope, who visited an exhibition of Native American craft work in Washington DC in 1827.

Reservation life

Source 11 shows another tragic result of government policy: Native people herded together on RESERVATIONS. Many Native people were forcibly moved from their homelands and settled on reservations. The Cherokees from Georgia, for example, were forced to march over 1,300 kilometres along the 'Trail of Tears' in 1838 to 1839. Usually, the land on the reservations was too poor for farming, there was no game to hunt, and nothing for Native people to do. The government provided RATIONS and makeshift housing but, not surprisingly, many people became ill and depressed, and thousands died.

Killing a culture

Native American children were taken away from reservations and made to attend schools like the one in Source 12. They were taught to forget their own culture and were beaten if they spoke Native languages. They were trained to 'fit in' with European-American ways. This policy wrecked many young lives. On leaving school, the children found they were misfits. They were no longer 'real' Native people, with traditional beliefs and skills, but they could never be accepted as equals by whites.

Other schools were run by missionaries. Although many of these men and women had good intentions, they were sometimes feared and disliked.

Even well-meaning, well-educated people sometimes failed to appreciate Native American culture. Like the British traveller quoted in Source 13, they thought that the best thing to do was to help Native Americans forget their past. They wanted to teach Native Americans new skills, so they could join the modern, 'progressive' civilisation now ruling their land.

SOURCE 14
A Crow Native American family in their European-style home in Montana, 1910.

SOURCE 15
A member of the Warm Springs Native people on duty as a US Army scout in 1873.

Forced to conform?

Around 1900, it looked as if Native American civilisation would soon be dead, and its traditions forgotten. It seemed that Native Americans would have to fit in with European-American lifestyles or face a life of poverty and despair. Many Native Americans, like the middle-class family in Source 14, made the choice to fit in. Some Native Americans joined the US Army or worked as government scouts. You can see one of them in Source 15.

Today, it might seem sad that people abandoned their traditional Native American ways. But is that a sentimental view? Is it similar to the attitude held by European-Americans at the beginning of this century and illustrated by the photograph in Source 16? That picture of a 'noble' Native American was carefully posed by a white photographer, using a man chosen for his good looks. The man is dressed in borrowed clothes and stands in a dramatic landscape which is not his home. Historians have commented that admiring images of Native American people, like Source 16, only became widespread once Native American culture had been destroyed.

SOURCE 16
A romantic portrait taken by Joseph Kossuth Dixon, a European-American photographer.

attainment target 1

1 Look back at the earlier pages in this unit. Make a list of all the different reasons why Native American civilisation was almost completely destroyed during the 19th century.

2 Which reason do you think was most important?

3 Which reasons do you think were the fault of the government, and which were the fault of individual Americans?

4 Do you think wars could have been avoided if government policy had been different?

5 Do you think Native American civilisation had any chance of survival?

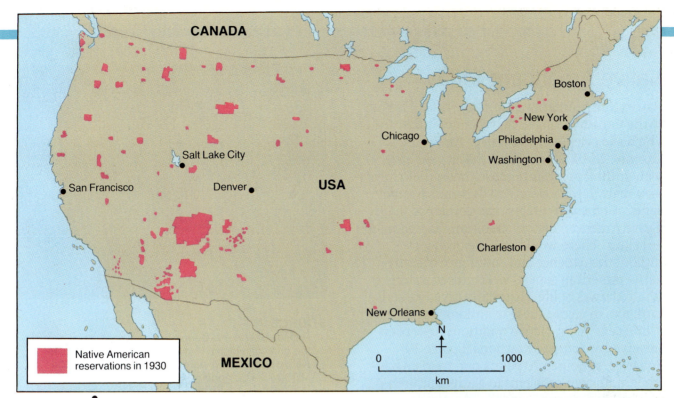

CANADA

Boston
New York
Chicago
Philadelphia
Washington
Salt Lake City
San Francisco
Denver
USA
Charleston
New Orleans
N
MEXICO
0   1000
km

SOURCE 17
This map shows remaining Native American lands around 1930.

Second-class citizens

Native American men and women who wanted the best for themselves and their children were forced to conform. Unless they became like European-Americans, Native peoples were confined to the reservations (Source 17). They were deprived of their right to live and work freely in their homelands, and had to rely on government welfare handouts. Disease, alcoholism and ILLITERACY were widespread. A few Native Americans left the reservations to find work in cities or on farms. But without proper education or training, they were confined to dead-end jobs.

Anyone who wanted to protest against this situation found that Native people had few civil rights. In 1871, the US government had removed independent status from Native nations. As early as 1831, they had been described as 'communities dependent on the United States'. Native American people – the first Americans – were not given full CITIZENSHIP until 1924. Government welfare organisations talked about the 'the Indian Problem'. They did not realise that racial prejudice and discrimination was a problem for society as a whole, as Source 18 shows. Can any society be proud of itself unless it treats **all** its citizens with fairness and justice?

SOURCE 18
This photograph shows a public meeting of the racist movement, the Ku Klux Klan, in West Virginia, 1924.

ACTIVITY

Look at the final sentence in the text on this page. Work with a small group to discuss the question raised there. Do you agree that 'no society can be proud of itself unless it treats all its citizens with fairness and justice'? Share the results of your discussion with other members of your class.

Native Americans today

'Native North American Me' is the title of a song by the Canadian singer, Buffy Sainte-Marie, in which she celebrates her Native American ancestry. In 1900, songs like that would have been unthinkable. Since those times, there have been many legal actions and demands for civil rights. A renewed interest has developed in Native American history, traditions, ceremonies and skills. These would all have been lost without the patience and endurance of some Native American ELDERS who refused to forget their old ways of life. Historians have worked hard, too, to record these testimonies of the past.

In recent years, Native traditions have been preserved as tourist attractions (Source 19). However, as Source 20 points out, tourism has brought its own problems to Native culture.

SOURCE 19

Many Native American craftworkers still make beautiful objects using traditional techniques.

'Our costumes are thought beautiful. But it's as if the person [who wears them] didn't exist.'

SOURCE 20

A comment made by Rigoberta Menchu, a Native South American from Guatemala. In 1992, she won the Nobel Peace Prize for her work for human rights.

1 Look at Source 19. Tourism and the HERITAGE INDUSTRY have become very popular (and profitable) in recent years. In time, they may pose new problems for the survival of 'real' Native American civilisation. Can you think what these problems might be? Source 20 gives you a clue.

SOURCE 21

Russell Means and Dennis Banks, two of the leaders of the American Indian Movement which campaigns for Native people's civil rights. They were photographed in 1973 with a European-American church leader.

Towards a better future

Today, there are campaigns which call for a new respect for all the Native nations in the world. Many people are ashamed of past racial prejudices. 'Green' campaigners share traditional Native American concern for the environment. Successes by recent Native American scholars, artists, poets, dancers, singers and writers have increased public awareness of Native people's skills. As Sources 21 and 22 show us, Native people are campaigning so that, one day, all members of their nations will be able to proclaim their identity with pride.

SOURCE 22

A wall-painting from Brooklyn, New York. Today, Native peoples from North and South America are still campaigning for justice and equality.

Glossary

Adventurers
People who travelled to distant lands, hoping to make their fortunes, usually through trade.

Ancestry
Another word for 'ancestors': the men and women a person is descended from.

Archaeologists
People who study past *civilisations* using physical remains such as buildings, landscape features, bones, pottery and many other kinds of objects to help them.

Buckskin
Fine, soft leather, made from the skin of a buck (a male deer).

Buffalo
A large, grass-eating, wild animal, related to the cow. Herds containing millions of buffalo once roamed the Great Plains of North America.

Canyons
Deep, steep valleys, formed by rivers which have cut their way through sandy rocks.

Caribou
A large wild animal, related to the deer, which lives in the cold arctic regions of North America. It feeds on moss.

Citizenship
Civil rights – being allowed to vote, to campaign and to stand for election to local and national government. Also being entitled to the same educational and welfare benefits as all other people living in your land.

Civilisations
Peoples or nations who share similar beliefs, lifestyles, languages, arts and crafts, traditions and histories.

Coniferous
Used to describe trees, usually evergreen, which produce cones containing seeds.

Continents
The great land-masses of the world: Africa, America, Asia, Australia, Europe.

Councils
Meetings where important matters were discussed and decisions affecting the community or nation were taken.

Coyote
A wild animal rather like a wolf.

Elders
A term of respect, used to describe old people.

Environments
People's surroundings. Used to describe landscape, climate, vegetation and wildlife.

Exotic
Unusual or coming from a distant place. Often also used to mean glamorous or exciting.

Grouse
A wild bird, about the size of a chicken, hunted for meat.

'Halfbreeds'
An old, offensive word used to describe people of mixed ethnic origins.

Heritage industry
Part of the tourist industry, which arranges visits to places of historic interest. It encourages people to enjoy an unreal, romanticised image of the past, rather than to study history thoughtfully.

Homelands
The place where people are born; an area occupied for a long time by one nation.

Idols
Objects (for example carvings or statues) that are worshipped.

Illiteracy
Being unable to read and write.

Innovation
A new idea or invention; a change that is made to the traditional way of doing things.

Kachina dolls
Small religious models – **not** playthings – used to teach children from the Hopi nation about Kachinas (powerful spirits).

Lemming
A small wild animal, rather like a rat, hunted for meat.

Lodges
Houses made of tightly-packed earth.

Massacre
Brutal killing of a large number of people.

Medicine bundles
Collections of objects, such as bones, stones and feathers, believed to have magical powers.

Mink
A wild animal, rather like an otter, with a beautiful glossy coat. Hunted for its fur.

Missionaries
People who travel to distant lands, aiming to win new believers for their own religion.

Mukluk boots
Warm, fur-lined boots, made of sealskin and coated with whale fat to make them waterproof.

Mule
An animal bred from a horse mated with a donkey. Mules are strong and can survive harsh conditions.

Myths
Ancient stories, often about magical or mysterious topics, which help people explain difficult subjects; for example, how the world was created, or why people fall in love.

Nomadic
With no fixed home; travelling in search of food, taking your living accommodation with you.

Overland trails
Long, dangerous routes leading from the settled eastern region of North America to the 'unknown' western territories.

Parkas
Long, hooded coats made of sealskin with a fox-fur lining and coated with whale fat for waterproofing.

Prairies
The vast, grassland region of central North America.

Puberty
The physical changes that take place when young people (usually teenagers) became adults.

Quill work
Decoration made of porcupine quills (spines). The quills were cleaned, dyed bright colours, flattened, and woven or sewn together.

Raids
Sudden attacks on enemies, aiming to capture men, women, horses or valuable goods.

Rations
Basic supplies of food, fuel and clothing.

Reservations
Land set aside by the US Government where Native Americans were forced to live.

Sacred
Holy.

Scalplocks
A piece of skin from the top of the head, with the hair still attached.

Settlers
People from Europe, or Americans of European ethnic origin, who moved westwards and took over Native peoples' lands.

Shamans
People who claimed to have magical healing powers.

Sinews
Tough, stringy parts of animal bodies, which attach muscles to bones. They were used as thread.

Stereotype
An artificial or exaggerated image.

Taboo
A religious rule.

Tipi
A nomad house, like a tent, made of *buffalo* skin.

Totem pole
Tall wooden posts, carved with faces of people and animals, often recording a family history.

Trance
A state of mind rather like a waking dream.

Treaties
Agreements made between nations.

Tubers
Swollen, underground parts of edible plants, for example, potatoes.

Tunics
Short, straight clothing, usually worn by men.

Vigils
Staying awake and keeping watch all night.

Index

Page numbers in **bold** refer to illustrations/captions

alcohol 43, 59
ancestry 25
Apache nation 21, **49**, **57**
Arapaho nation **51**
archaeologists 8–9

baskets **10**
beliefs 11, 25, 38–41, **50–51**
Black Elk **11**
Blackfeet nation 22, **25**
buckskin **34–35**
buffalo 8, **9–10**, 22, **45–46**, 56

ceremonies 29, **30**, 37–39, **37–39**, **50–51**
Cherokee nation 23
Cheyenne nation 22, **47**, 48
children 30, 32
climate 16, **18–23**, 36
clothes **6**, **13**, 34–37, **34–37**, 60
Columbus 52
Comanche nation 22, **28**, 31
community **27**, 39
co-operation 27
councils 26, **26**
cowboys 14
crafts **10–11**, 46, **57**, 60
Cree nation **7**, **15**, 22
Crow nation 22, 33

Delaware nation **14**
discrimination 14, **15**
disease 43, 59

environment **16–23**, 60
Erikson, Lief 52
Europeans 7, 12–15, 42–53

farming 17, **17**, 21–23
fishing 19
Folsom point 9, **9**
food 17–23
François I, King of France **12**
funerals 33
fur-trappers **43**

Geronimo (Goyathlay) 49, **49**
Great Basin 17, **20**, **31**, 36
Great Lakes **42**, 54
Great Plains 17, 22, 24–25, 28, **31**, 44
  buffalo **45**, 56
  tipi encampment **46**
Great Spirit **14**, **39**
guns 47, **47**

'halfbreeds' **15**
history **25**
homelands **24**, 28
Hopi nation 21, **27**, **32**, 33, 38, **50**
horses 44–46, **47**
hunters and gatherers 17–23
hunting grounds 25, 55
Huron nation **42**

Ice Age **8**, 9
illiteracy 59
Inuit nation 9, 17, 18, **36**, **39**
Iroquois nation **39**

jewellery **34**, 37, **37**, **45**

kachina dolls **11**
Kansa nation 22
kayaks 9
Ku Klux Klan **59**

landscapes 16–23
languages 25, 57
life cycles 30–31
Little Bighorn, battle of **54**
lodges 22

marriage 30, **31**, **37**
missionaries **14**, 50–51, 57
myths 11, 38

Natchez nation 23
nations 7, 24–41
Native, definition 6
Navajo nation **7**, 21, **30**, 38, **41**
Nez Percé nation **25**, **45**, **50**
Nobel Peace Prize **60**
nomads 8

old age 32–33, **32–33**
Old Bull **22**
ornaments **37**
overland trails **54**, 55

Paiute nation **6**, 20, **36**
Pawnee nation 22, **37**
peyote 51, **51**
pottery **10**
Powhatan **53**
prayers **30**, **39**
'progress' 56–57
puberty 30, **30**
Pueblo nation 21, **33**

racism **59**
railways 56, **56**
Red Cloud **6**, 7, **32**, 55
reservations 55, 57, **57**
rituals 38–41, **38–41**

scalplocks 28, **29**
schools **57**
shamans 26, 40–41, **40–41**
shelter 17–23
Shoshone nation 20, 30
Siberia 8, 9
Sioux nation **6**, 7, **11**, **14**, **15**, 22, **25**
  chiefs **6**, **22**, 28, **29**, **32**, **49**
  craft workers **46**
  wars **54–55**
Sitting Bull (Tatanka Yotanka) **28**
spear-heads 9, **9**
Standing Bear **48**
stereotypes 13, **15**

tipis **11**, **22–23**, 46, **46**
tools 9
totem poles 11, **11**
trade **42**, 43
treaties **49**, **52**, 53

United States Army **21**, **22**, **54**, 58
Ute nation **31**, 47

Vikings 52

wars **26**, 28–29, 47, **47**, 53–55, **53–55**
weapons **9**, **28**, 47
westerns 14, **15**
whales 17–18
wildlife 18–23
women 31–32, **31–32**
Wounded Knee, battle of **14**, 51, **55**

First published in 1993 by Collins Educational
A division of HarperCollins*Publishers*
77–85 Fulham Palace Road
Hammersmith
London W6 8JB

ISBN 0 00 327259 1

Cover design by Glynis Edwards
Book designed by Don Parry, Peartree Design Associates
Series planned by Nicole Lagneau
Edited by Helen Mortimer
Picture research by Celia Dearing
Artwork by Julia Osorno
Production by Mandy Inness

Typeset by Dorchester Typesetting Group Ltd, Dorset, UK

Printed and bound by Stige-Arti Grafiche, Italy

Acknowledgements

The publishers would like to thank Dr Colin Taylor for his comments on the typescript.

Every effort has been made to contact the holders of copyright material but if any have been inadvertently overlooked the publishers will be pleased to make the necessary arrangements at the first opportunity.

Photographs: The publishers would like to thank the following for permission to reproduce photographs on these pages:

T = top, B = bottom, R = right, C = centre, L = left

B&C Alexander 9T; Courtesy of the Arizona Historical Society Acc 20602 49T; National Museum of American Art/Art Resource 13R, 22TR, 26, 27, 31, 34R, 37, 40B; Associated Press 60T; The Bridgeman Art Library/British Museum, London 12, Alecto Historical Editions 29, National Army Museum 43R, Smithsonian Institution 44, Private Collection 46T; Chicago Historical Society 36B; All rights reserved, photo archives, Denver Museum of Natural History 9C; E.T. Archive 13L, 17, 23C; Werner Forman Archive/Maxwell Museum of Anthropology 9B, WFA 10L, Schindler Collection NY 38R, Provincial Museum of BC Canada 39BR, Plains Indian Museum 50; Glenbow Archives, Calgary Canada 35L, 38L, 40T; Robert Harding Picture Library/Walter Rawlings 11L, 19TR, Ian Robertson 18TL, Adam Woolfitt 21R, Nedra Westwater 23T, Rockefeller Collection 52, RHPL 60B; The Hutchison Library 11R, Robert Francis 19TL, Bernard Régent 20TL, John Downman 22TL; Kansas State Historical Society 56; The Kobal Collection 15; Library of Congress 32, 59; Johnston, Francis B. "Class in American History", plate from an album of Hampton Institute 1899–1900 platinum print 7½ × 9½ The Museum of Modern Art NY Gift of Lincoln Kirstein 57B; National Museum of the American Indian 10TR, 10BR, 41, 43L, 45T, 46B; Nebraska State Historical Society 48L; Peter Newark's Western Americana 3, 13B; Courtesy the Edward E. Ayer Collection, the Newberry Library 28B; New York State Historical Association, Cooperstown 14R; Courtesy New York State Library 47T; State Museum of History, Oklahoma Historical Society 30L; Phoebe Hurst Museum of Anthropology, the University of California at Berkeley 25; Rex Features 7B, 60C; Smithsonian Institution photo 3237a 6L, 1653 6R, 2437 7T, 76-6515 11B, 55018 14L, 57234 18TR, 55019 18B, 42975-A 19B, 1641 20TR, 1547 20B, 1878-B 21L, 3179-B-6 22B, 482-A 23B, 3197-A 28T, 1713 30R, 42019-A 33, 3120-A 34L, 1632 35R, 56720 36T, 1623 36C, 43114A 39L, 2374 39TR, 56528 47B, 79-4274 48R, 456 49BL, 55054 49BR, 1458 51T, 81-9626 51BL, 1456-D 51BR, 4700 54, 76-6091 57T, 4644 58TL, 56496 58TR, 83-7819 58B.

Cover photograph: Peter Newark's Western Americana

The author and publishers gratefully acknowledge the following publications from which written sources in this book are drawn:

Bantam Doubleday Dell for an extract from A. M. Josephy Junior, *The Indian Heritage of America*, Alfred A. Knopf (New York) 1968; Facts on File for an extract from *The Atlas of the North American Indian*, Carl Waldmann, Facts on File (New York) 1974; *The Guardian* for an extract in an article by Michael Reid in *The Guardian*, 17 October 1992; Harper and Row for extracts from J. D. Jennings et al. (eds.), *The Native Americans*, 2nd edition, Harper and Row (New York) 1977 and for an extract from W. E. Washburn, *The Indian in America*, Harper and Row (New York) 1975; Professor Nancy Lurie and Waveland Press, Inc. for extracts from E. B. Leacock and N. O. Lurie, *North American Indians in Historical Perspective*, Random House (New York) 1971; Reprinted with the permission of Macmillan Publishing Company an extract from *The Long Death: The Last Days of the Plains Indians*, Ralph K. Andrist © 1964 by Ralph K. Andrist; Penguin Books Ltd for extracts from George Catlin, *North American Indians*, edited by Peter Mathiessen, Penguin (London) 1989; Reprinted by permission of the Peters, Fraser & Dunlop Group Ltd, extracts from Dee Brown, *Bury My Heart At Wounded Knee*, Random Century, 1991; For an extract published in *Hearts & Hands* by Pat Ferrero, Elaine Hedges and Julie Silber. The Quilt Digest Press, 1987. Used by permission; Simon & Schuster for extracts from J. Gattuso (ed), *Insight Guides – Native America*, Prentice Hall (New Jersey) 1991; Time Life Inc. for an extract from Benjamin Capp and the Editors of Time-Life Books, *The Old West: The Great Chiefs*, Time-Life Books, 1975; For extracts reprinted from *Black Elk Speaks*, by John G. Neihardt, by permission of the University of Nebraska Press. Copyright 1932, 1959, 1972, by John G. Neihardt. Copyright © 1961 by the John G. Neihardt Trust; For extracts reprinted from *American Indian Women: Telling Their Lives*, by Gretchen M. Bataille and Kathleen Mullen Sands, by permission of the University of Nebraska Press. Copyright 1984 by the University of Nebraska Press.